# R.N. KAO

# R.N. KAO
# GENTLEMAN
# SPYMASTER

## NITIN A. GOKHALE

B L O O M S B U R Y

NEW DELHI • LONDON • OXFORD • NEW YORK • SYDNEY

BLOOMSBURY INDIA
Bloomsbury Publishing India Pvt. Ltd
Second Floor, LSC Building No. 4
DDA Complex, Pocket C – 6 & 7
Vasant Kunj, New Delhi 110070

BLOOMSBURY, BLOOMSBURY INDIA and the Diana logo are
trademarks of Bloomsbury Publishing Plc

First published 2019
This edition published 2019

ISBN: 978-93-89449-28-0

6 8 10 9 7 5

Printed and bound in India by Replika Press Pvt Ltd

To find out more about our authors and books visit www.bloomsbury.com and
sign up for our newsletters

*To all unnamed*
*and faceless R&AW sleuths*

# Contents

# Foreword

This initiative of the Research & Analysis Wing (R&AW) to publish the memoirs of its founding father, Rameshwar Nath Kao, is a pioneering effort that needs to be commended.

For any member of India's intelligence community, it would be a cherished ambition to be called upon to write a foreword for a book on one of its tallest doyens Ramji Kao, as he was known to his friends, relatives and well-wishers. I am no exception.

Ramji Kao straddled the world of secret intelligence during India's formative years as a nation. Deputed to the Intelligence Bureau (IB) in 1947 and trained under the watchful eyes of the legendary Bhola Nath Mullick post-Independence, Mr Kao emerged as an institution builder par excellence, and an epitome of professional excellence and exemplary personal conduct. Humble, suave, intellectual and modest, Ramji Kao left an indelible imprint on anyone he met or interacted with.

His exploits are legendary. Whether it was the professionalism with which he conducted the 'Kashmir Princess' probe in the mid-1950s or his contributions to the liberation of Bangladesh in 1971 or his role in ensuring Sikkim's merger with India, Kao always brought to bear his sage counsel and leadership qualities to deliver desired results.

Ramji Kao also had many firsts to his credit. A close adviser and security chief to three Indian Prime Ministers, he was one of the founding fathers of the Directorate General of Security (DGS) in the aftermath of the disastrous Sino-Indian conflict of 1962.

Later, he went on to head, as the first Chief, the Aviation Research Centre (ARC) and the Research & Analysis Wing (R&AW)—two of India's foremost intelligence agencies that were created in the 1960s. It is a fitting tribute to his leadership skills that within three years of the creation of the R&AW in September 1968, the organisation went on to play a sterling role in the Indo-Pakistan War of 1971.

A multi-talented genius, Ramji Kao also pursued his passions in the artistic and creative fields. Being a quintessential sculptor—'he was good with wood, clay and stone', according to the author—it is no surprise that he used this talent to curate some of the finest intelligence organisations in Independent India's history. He also mentored two generations of R&AW sleuths, many of whom have come to be known as 'Kaoboys'. Those who worked with him swear by his human qualities, eye for detail, meticulous grooming and affable nature.

What is less known about Ramji Kao is the fact that he had meticulously recorded for posterity his reminiscences in a tape recorder. He even corrected the transcripts, but with the proviso that these tapes should be gradually opened to the public after his death.

I am happy that finally Kao's work is being organised in the form of a biography. Written by the well-known strategic affairs analyst and author, Nitin A. Gokhale, it is a worthy tribute to the man who nurtured important institutions through their fledgling years. Gokhale, who has an impressive body of work on national security affairs, has aptly captured the professional journey of Kao and simultaneously flagged the key milestones in the R&AW's journey so far.

Personally blessed by Ramji Kao's 99-year-old wife, Malini Kao, I am sure this book will be read with great interest not only by intelligence professionals but also by common citizens in the years to come.

September 2019 **Ajit Doval**
*National Security Adviser*
*New Delhi*

# Preface

Where does one begin to chronicle the life and times of a colossus like Rameshwar Nath Kao? Does one begin with his greatest moment of glory in contributing to the liberation of East Pakistan and the formation of Bangladesh in 1971? Or the fact that he was the founder of one of the world's best spy agencies, the R&AW? Does one talk about his fiercely private personality? Or his wide-ranging contacts in the secretive world of espionage? For an author like me, it had to be a combination of the personal and the professional to try and capture the essence of Kao, the man, the legend.

Somewhere deep in the archives of the Nehru Memorial Museum and Library (NMML), in the heart of New Delhi, lies a set of papers that researchers and historians interested in recording the history of Indian intelligence would love to get their hands on. Alas, only part of those papers—transcripts of tape-recorded dictations left behind by Kao—are currently available. Three crucial files on Bangladesh, the merger of Sikkim and Mrs Indira Gandhi's assassination will not be open until 2025, according to instructions left behind by him, months before he passed away in January 2002.

Since those tapes and papers are not public, this biography of Rameshwar Nath Kao—RNK or 'Ramji' to his friends, colleagues and family—had to depend on the personal memories of a vast array of individuals who knew him in different capacities and their interpretation of his personality and contribution, apart from his correspondence with varied intelligence professionals.

The task was made doubly difficult by the fact that Kao was by nature a very private person. He was rarely photographed. Except for a tape-recoded interview to Pupul Jayakar, one of Mrs Indira Gandhi's closest friends, RNK is not known to have given any public statements or formal interviews with any journalist. So, when I was requested to undertake this task, it seemed impossible. But thanks to help proffered by the Kao family, the three personal files of Kao that are now open for researchers and scholars at the NMML, the P.N. Haksar papers and R&AW's former officers—some of them retired as chiefs of the organisation—I was able to put together this first full account of the personal and professional journey of Ramji Kao—the sensitive, compassionate man behind the façade of a distant, stern spymaster.

Not everyone who made this book possible can be named but some who can be are: Shakti Sinha, Director of NMML, for his generous and quick cooperation in locating and making available the Kao files; Vikram Sood, former R&AW Chief, himself an author, for his timely and critical interventions in reading the early draft of the manuscript; Vappala Balachandran, former R&AW officer, prolific writer and columnist for sharing copies of his correspondence with RNK and recounting some important anecdotes about him; my colleagues in BharatShakti.in and sniwire.com, the two digital platforms I own and run; Soumitra 'Bobby' Banerjee, my former boss in early days of my journalism career (for reasons which will become apparent when you read the book in detail); the most supportive team of Paul Kumar, Jyoti Mehrotra, Rajbilochan Prasad and Satyabrat Mishra of Bloomsbury; and, last but not least, the Kao family.

The book however has become possible only because my wife Neha and our sons, Harsh and Utkarsh, who have put up with my crazy schedule of writing 10–12 hours a day at a stretch for two months. During this period, I cancelled a pre-scheduled foreign trip with my wife, going to movies was put on hold and family dinners became a hurried affair in the race to meet the deadline. It is their support that allows me to function stress-free when I am doing projects with the tightest deadlines imaginable.

Finally, I can't thank National Security Adviser Ajit Doval enough for penning the foreword. It is a rare honour to write the untold story of the iconic R.N. Kao, and to have Mr Doval, another legend in the world of intelligence, introduce the book is a double privilege.

One last word. This is neither history nor a detective thriller. It is by no means a comprehensive chronicle of the R&AW either. Just read it for what it is: a short glimpse into how organisations tasked to protect India's national interests took shape. Many have contributed in the making of this book but the shortcomings are entirely because of me.

September 2019 **Nitin A. Gokhale**
*New Delhi*

# Prologue

February 2019: Days before the Indian Air Force (IAF) planes bombed the Balakot camp of the Jaish-e-Mohammad (JeM), in Pakistan's Khyber Pakhtunkhwa Province, two assets of the Research and Analysis Wing (R&AW)—India's foreign intelligence agency—had managed to get inside the Balakot facility for a week between 15 and 22 February and send vivid details that clinched the decision to hit the camp that trained recruits for jihad in Jammu and Kashmir.

The intelligence showed that the training camp was alive and kicking, and was, in fact, getting ready to welcome 150 more trainees from 25 February. The two sources managed to document the entire facility visually and identify important buildings and their occupants. Spread over six acres, the camp had 10 major buildings or complexes devoted to various kinds of activities. Most importantly, the camp was run by JeM Chief Masood Azhar's brother-in-law Yusuf Azhar, who resided in an abandoned school complex on the campus.

On 26 February, this real-time information allowed Prime Minister Narendra Modi to order a strike deep inside Pakistani territory, forever erasing the unspoken fear in the minds of Indian decision-makers of triggering an unintended military escalation with Pakistan.

**Flashback to May 1999:** Pakistan's then Chief of Army Staff, General Pervez Musharraf, was on a visit to China when the Kargil conflict was just about beginning to make news in India and Pakistan. R&AW operatives were on the prowl to get as much intelligence as possible. They hit pay dirt on 25–26 May.

Musharraf was speaking to his Chief of General Staff, Lt General Mohammed Aziz, from Beijing on an open line. The R&AW was listening in. Aziz reported to Musharraf about a meeting chaired by (Prime Minister) Nawaz Sharif at which the chiefs of the Pakistani Air Force and Navy complained to Sharif that Musharraf had kept them in the dark about the invasion of Kargil heights. R&AW records the conversation and after much deliberation, India hands over the evidence to Nawaz to convince him of Pakistan Army and Musharraf's perfidy in Kargil.

**December 1971:** R&AW's number two, K Sankaran Nair, gets advance information from a mole he had planted in the office of Gen Yahya Khan, then Pakistan's dictator, about a plan to carry out a pre-emptive strike on Indian airfields and IAF fleets stationed close to the border. Nair alerts IAF, preventing a catastrophe. Pakistan's air strike fails. India joins the war, routs Pakistan in 13 days, liberates Bangladesh and the rest, as they say, is history.

These are just three examples of strategic intelligence that shaped and changed the course of the Indian subcontinent's recent history. In each case, it was the R&AW which provided the input, rising to the occasion when called to do so. In exactly half a century, the R&AW has proved its worth time and again.

This saga of R&AW's formation and especially of the life and times of its founder, the legendary Rameshwar Nath (R.N.) Kao, Ramji to his friends, RNK to others, has never been fully understood. In its 51st year of existence, the story of R&AW and its founder, RNK, was waiting to be told.

Read on.

ONE

# Not an Easy Start

In the late 19th and the early 20th centuries, there was something about the Allahabad[1]–Banaras[2] region in the erstwhile United Provinces of British India that attracted a lot of Kashmiri Pandits to either settle down or study there. The most famous residents of Allahabad were, of course, the Nehrus.

Motilal Nehru made his name and wealth in Allahabad before joining the Indian National Congress (INC). His son, Jawaharlal Nehru, was the most well-known resident of Allahabad. But there were many other Kashmiri Pandits who had migrated from Jammu and Kashmir and made the Allahabad–Banaras region their home and *karmabhumi* (land where one works).

---

[1] Present-day Prayagraj.
[2] Present-day Varanasi.

One of the most distinguished civil servants of India, P.N. Haksar, studied there as a college student between 1929 and 1935. Another young Kashmiri Brahmin, who was two or three years junior to Haksar, was also educating himself at the Allahabad University. This young Kashmiri was Rameshwar Nath Kao (RNK), the legendary spymaster, widely known as the founder of India's external espionage agency, the Research and Analysis Wing (R&AW). Years later, the duo, Kao and Haksar, would play a seminal role in liberating East Pakistan and in the formation of Bangladesh—Haksar as Principal Secretary to Prime Minister Indira Gandhi and R.N. Kao as the Head of R&AW, which would form in 1968, barely three years earlier to the Bangladesh Liberation War.

Haksar and Kao were destined to work together, not the least because they belonged to a small but very influential Kashmiri Brahmin community in central India, who had kinship with and access to the Nehru family. Both, however, rose in their respective professions because they were thorough in their jobs and men of great integrity, who did not hesitate to offer the correct advice even if it was unpalatable to their political bosses.

Kao's ancestor, Pandit Ghasi Ram Kao, was originally a resident of Srinagar district in the Kashmir Valley. He left the Kashmir Valley in the beginning of the 18th century in search of a job, and landed in Delhi with his son, Pandit Damodar Das Kao, and other family members. Dr B.N. Sharga, a Kashmiri Pandit himself, has traced the migration of Kashmiri Brahmins to different parts of India, and has written a magnum opus in Hindi called *Kashmiri Panditon*

*Ke Anmol Ratna*, which is a six-volume work on the family histories of several thousand non-resident Kashmiri Pandits. He has written extensively about Kao's lineage as well.

According to Dr Sharga, Pandit Ghasi Ram Kao's younger son, Pandit Daya Nidhan Kao, went to Oudh from Delhi during the rule of Nawab Asaf-ud-Daula (1775–1797) and became a dewan in his court. He settled down with his family in the Kashmiri Mohalla of Lucknow, where he built two houses. The Kao family flourished in Oudh and many of the family members became leading citizens in Lucknow, where they obtained education. As the family grew, they spread themselves across Oudh, which later became a part of the United Provinces.

In the late 1870s, RNK's grandfather, Pandit Kedar Nath Kao, after completing his education, became a deputy collector under the British and lived in Ramnagar, Banaras, for quite some time. He got married at 43 to a lady who was then 16 years of age. She bore him two sons—Triloki Nath Kao and Dwarika Nath Kao. RNK's father was the younger of the two brothers. The two brothers were very close to each other.

Triloki Nath Kao became a chemist and shifted from Lucknow to Baroda, whereas his younger brother, Dwarika Nath Kao, became a deputy collector like his father. Triloki Nath Kao married Daya Shuri Zutshi, who was the daughter of Shambhu Nath Zutshi of Lucknow. He lived till the age of about 84 and passed away in Calcutta in November 1976.

Dwarika Nath Kao was married to Khemwati Kaul, who was the daughter of Srikishan Kaul of Lahore. Two sons,

Rameshwar Nath Kao and Shyam Sunder Nath Kao, were born to this couple. The younger brother was, in fact, born a couple of months after the passing away of the father at the age of 24 years old. Rameshwar Nath Kao, according to his own notes, was born on 10 May 1918 in an old colonial-type bungalow in Banaras cantonment. His father, who then was about 29 years old, was working as a recruiting officer during the closing months of the First World War. From the account that RNK heard later, his father was a fastidious person. He also seemed to have had literary pretensions, because RNK remembered having seen at least one poem in Urdu that his father had written in aid of the recruitment drive for the British Government of India.

RNK wrote, 'My father, soon after my birth, was appointed as a deputy collector in Uttar Pradesh, then known as the UP-Civil Service. His father, that is my grandfather, had also held a similar post, having started life as a naib-tahsildar. By the time of his retirement, he had been promoted to deputy collector, which in the atmosphere then prevailing, was regarded as a high pinnacle of achievement.' In later years, the Kao family lost their roots in Lucknow and made different homes wherever the exigencies of service took the family.

RNK noted, 'My childhood seems to have been overshadowed by the fact that my father died prematurely at the age 29, when I was five. The result was that my mother became a widow at the age of 25. The passing away of my father at an early age was the tragedy from which my family, which was quite small, did not entirely recover, and it certainly coloured my entire outlook during my childhood days, which was rather cheerless and lonely.' RNK, still a six-year-old child, was taken to Baroda by his uncle Triloki Nath Kao, who used to run a chemical factory. With short breaks, RNK spent many years of his boyhood in Baroda High school. Naturally, he picked up Gujarati. His uncle brought up a large family, which included three sons and three daughters of his own, along with RNK and his brother. They all lived together. So, he had plenty of playmates in the house itself. However, as his uncle's business faltered in Baroda, RNK's mother took the two children to Unnao where her brothers lived. But after a year in Unnao, the family moved to Banaras, where RNK was admitted in the sixth grade in the Theosophical High School at Kamacha.

In Banaras, the family were the tenants of a prominent local citizen called Babu Durga Prasad. RNK recalled, 'As a child, he seemed to me, in many ways, a kind of a Renaissance man. He was rich, had a deep and abiding interest in Indian classical music and played string instruments with a high degree of virtuosity. He was also a sculptor of sorts and had helped to build a marble relief map of India. In addition to these, he had a hobby of repairing old clocks and I remember that the top floor of his house was full of old clocks, some of which must have been master pieces.' One does not know—and RNK does not mention it anywhere—of his own interest in fine arts, especially sculpting, was inspired by his short stay in Babu Durga Prasad's house.

However, after a year of schooling in Banaras, the family moved back to Baroda since RNK's grandparents were getting on in years. The unsettled and uncertain life in his childhood and the early loss of his father appears to have had a lasting impact on RNK's life. Moreover, his experiences in school—a majority of them being unpleasant—appear to have shaped RNK's personality in adulthood, as he himself has recorded in his notes, which is now archived at the Nehru Memorial Museum and Library (NMML) in New Delhi.[3] He wrote, 'In Baroda, at the beginning, I had a pretty wretched time at school. I did not know the local language. My knowledge of Gujarati was elementary, with the result that all communication with my fellow classmates and other boys had to be in English, which acted as a strong restricting influence. Also, at this stage, my body had grown fat. I remember, when I was 11 or 12 years old, I weighed nearly 120 pounds. This was a subject of ridicule for my classmates on innumerable occasions in the school, apart from being ragged for my name 'Kao', which was invariably mispronounced as 'Cow'. I was also ridiculed for my large body size. The nicknames given to me at school were brown buffalo, sack of potatoes and things like that. I was sensitive about this and tended to withdraw into my own shell, which, I think, laid the foundations of an introspective withdrawn approach to life in general.'

He went on to add, 'I remember, day after day my mother used to give me money to eat at the school canteen, but I just could not bring myself to go to the canteen and buy it. So, on several occasions, I remember that a servant was sent to accompany me, who used to buy food for me in the restaurant or canteen. I could only eat then. In some ways, this shyness about being seen eating in public has persisted with me, and I

---

[3] R.N. Kao papers, serial No. 2, NMML, New Delhi.

am still ill at ease while eating at a wayside restaurant or eating food offered by a street side hawker.'

RNK also acknowledged that his close family had the biggest influence on him. He listed his family members in order of their importance in his life—his mother, his father because of his personality and his amiable nature, his uncle and, finally, his grandparents, particularly his grandmother.

Despite the premature death of his father, RNK—who recorded his memoirs in the late 1970s—appeared to have retained several memories, although very vague, about his father. 'I have a faint impression, confirmed from some photographs that I saw later, that my father was a large man. He dressed carefully and had the reputation of being extremely neat and clean in his turnout. The earliest remembrance I have is at Mathura, where my father was posted as a deputy collector and we were living in a house on the banks of the Yamuna. One of the earliest impressions that I have about my father is that he was an early riser and I have a mental picture of him shaving by the light of a kerosene lantern.'

However, a painful memory about his father also stayed forever with RNK. 'He was suffering from some stomach disorder and though he was a large and a powerfully built man, his body dissolved in about three months and he died prematurely. In the last stages of his illness, I remember that though he was posted in a town called Hardoi, he was taken to Lucknow for treatment and we were living in a flat on the first floor. In that flat, I remember to have spent many, many lonely and sad evenings, when I used to be in the verandah watching the people go by in the street below. My father was then dangerously ill; strict silence was enjoined on me and being the only child, I had no playmate. So, there was nothing that I could do except to watch the passing scene in the street below,' RNK recalled.

Throughout the difficult period of India of the 1920s and the 1930s, the Kao family faced a lot of financial hardships as RNK's uncle suffered losses in his business time and again. RNK's fortunes, along with his brother and mother, ebbed and flowed with the state of his uncle's business. In 1932, RNK's uncle changed his line of business and became associated with a cement factory, which had been established in Andheri near Bombay[4]. As the grandparents were dead, the whole family then shifted to Bombay, where they stayed in a bungalow in Santa Cruz. Within a year, however, RNK's uncle's fortune suffered another reverse. 'The establishment at Bombay was broken up. My mother and my aunt went to their respective brothers, my uncle shifted to a small lodging and my cousin and I went to live for one year in a hostel run by the Ramakrishna Mission in Villa Parle, which is a suburb of Bombay,' RNK wrote.

While at the Ramakrishna Hostel, RNK developed interest in yoga since he felt a strong desire to overcome his obesity. His one-year stay at Ramakrishna Mission deepened this interest. Yoga gradually cured him of obesity. RNK also remembered that during this period, he read, for the first time, some of Swami Vivekananda's works, particularly his Raja Yoga. The habit of doing yoga that he picked up at

---

[4] Present-day Mumbai.

Ramakrishna Mission incidentally stayed with RNK till the end of his life.

As the financial position of the family worsened, RNK and his cousin could not continue their studies in Bombay. So, they returned to Uttar Pradesh. Both got admission in the Lucknow University for their bachelor's degree, with RNK also securing a room in the Mehmoodabad Hostel.

This is where Kao's life seemed to look up, according to his own recollection. He took up English Literature, Indian History and Persian for his bachelor's. He decided to specialise in Ancient Indian History. 'The study of this period of our country's developments opened up an absolutely new vista before me. It gripped my interest which has, in a manner of speaking, lasted till today, and this further developed into an interest in the critical study of temple architecture and statues. In later years, as a corollary of my interest in statues, I took up clay modelling too. My stay of two years in Lucknow University from where I graduated in 1936, was quite eventful externally, but it marked a new phase in my academic life as for the first time, I discovered that I had some felicity for writing and speaking English, at least at the undergraduate level. This won me encomiums and compliments from my teachers and at the end of my graduation, they encouraged me to join the master's programme in English Literature at Allahabad University,' RNK wrote.

In Allahabad, the only luxury RNK had allowed himself was a weekly visit to the cinema, which in those days, with students' concessions, cost only 9 annas. His mother gave him a monthly allowance of ₹50. RNK noted that this included

₹ 12 as tuition fee, ₹ 8 for the hostel room and ₹ 30 for living expenses. As he could not even afford a bicycle in those days, most evenings RNK used to either sit in the room and continue to study or go out for a short walk. He had developed some interest in hockey and occasionally played volleyball and basketball. Simultaneously, RNK had started working for competitive exams. He recalled, 'I was, at that time, working very hard preparing for the competitive examinations. My practice was to get up at 3 AM and work with short breaks throughout the day. The only luxury I allowed myself was about an hour's bicycle ride (on a borrowed cycle) in the evening, along with a cinema show once a week. In fact, I was so short of money that mostly I skipped the afternoon tea.'

While studying English Literature, RNK recalled, he seemed to have at last found his métier. 'My weekly visit to the cinema also became a part of the process of absorbing as much English as I could, because invariably I went to watch English movies, and when I use the word 'English', it includes those made by MGM and Hollywood. But I remember that in those days, actors and actresses like Greta Garbo, Jennith MacDonald, Fredrik Mash and Robert Tailor made a great impact on my youthful mind.'

About this time, RNK also developed some interest in joining the debates, on various subjects, which used to be held at Allahabad University. Gradually, somewhat to his own surprise, RNK discovered that he had the ability to put across his views cogently. 'The high watermark of my achievement was in 1939, when at the inter-University debate in Allahabad, I secured the first prize,' RNK wrote.

In 1938, RNK completed his master's degree in English Literature, securing the first position in the university. 'My recollection is that this was a very exciting moment for me, and I had a heady feeling with the stimulation of a solid achievement,' RNK noted. After all, he had won two gold medals for standing first in class. 'It was one of the proudest moments of my life. And for some reason, when I went up to the dais to receive the medal, the thought of my dead grandmother was uppermost in my mind. This was so, because she had exercised a great influence on my mind in my childhood. I recall endless number of evenings when I used to sit along with her other grandchildren by her bedside and listen to the stories about ancient heroes and great warriors, whose exploits have been enumerated in our scriptures, with which she regaled us ,' RNK recalled.

The success of his MA seemed sweeter for Kao since two years prior to that, his mother had asked him to find a job as most of the money that his late father had left behind had been exhausted. RNK recalled that he argued vigorously with his mother and insisted in obtaining a post-graduate degree. As he remembered, 'This suggestion (of taking up a job) I firmly rejected because I argued with my mother that a couple of thousand rupees or a little more would not see me through my life, that those were the important years and that it would be best if I invested this money by studying further. In the event, this proved to be the correct decision, though, of course, at that time, it was a bit of a plunge in the dark, because after I had done my MA and nearly finished my two years of law, all that was left between me and the wolf was ₹500. So, it was, in some ways, a miracle that I managed to get into the Indian Police, and that happened just before I had finished my law (final) lecture classes. But that is another story.'

It was during his stint at the Law College when RNK got his first glimpse of Jawaharlal Nehru. As he wrote, 'The first time I saw Pandit Jawaharlal Nehru was, I think, in 1936, when the plenary session of the INC was being held at Lucknow. He had probably just returned from Europe after Kamala Nehru's death. And my recollection is that I was much impressed with his sensitive, vibrant face. After that, I remember to have had two or three meetings with Pandit Jawaharlal Nehru in Allahabad in connection with the affairs of the students' union of the university there. While I was pursuing law, I got somewhat deeply involved with the affairs of the Allahabad University Students' Union and campaigned vigorously in favour of a friend of mine, called Billu Bhatnagar, who was finally elected as the president of the University Union.' As a reward, for his vigorous campaigning, RNK was nominated to the Executive Committee of the Students' Union.

Another distinct recollection that RNK has about his student days in Law College was of communal politics that was practiced even at the level of students' union. He recalled, 'While serving as a member of the Executive Committee, I got my first taste of the manner in which communal politics led to aberrations and endless discussions involving people, who otherwise seemed perfectly rational and normal. One of the questions being considered by the Executive Committee at that time was whether the National Flag should be hoisted over the union building or not. This was strongly opposed by a representative of the Muslim hostel, who said that either there should be no flag or that if the INC flag was hoisted, so should the Muslim League flag side by side. All of us argued vehemently that while the Congress flag was the National Flag, representing all communities in India, the Muslim League could not claim that its flag represented anyone else other than its Muslim supporters.'

Incidentally, the person who then represented the Muslim hostel in these debates was a person called Gufran. In Kao's memory, he was a tall, gangling youth with a broad face. 'My impression is that his family belongs from Azamgarh. Many years later, I learnt that his elder brother, Brig Usman, became a war hero, when in 1947 he was killed in Kashmir, fighting the Pakistan raiders. Our friend, Gurfan, himself had later joined the Army and elected to stay on in India. When I met him next, he was a Lt. Col and was working as an Assistant Military Secretary to the President,' Kao wrote. Brig Mohammad Usman, incidentally, commanded the 50 Para Brigade and is known as the Sher of Nowshera for his heroic exploits to defend Nowshera in Jammu and Kashmir (J&K) in 1947. He was awarded India's second highest gallantry award, the Maha Vir Chakra, posthumously.

By 1939, RNK finished his first year in law. Kao was 21 and could now appear for the competitive exams to join the Indian Police (IP), the forerunner of the current Indian Police Service (IPS). This is where RNK's life took a turn for the better.

# TWO

# Joining the IP, Shifting to IB

In the summer of 1939, RNK, having passed the written exam for entering the IP, was called for an interview. In those days, the interviews (also known as viva voce) used to be conducted by the Federal Public Service Commission Board. Kao distinctly remembered that the interview was held in the Council House of the UP-Government Secretariat in Lucknow.

The chairman of the board was an Englishman. According to his recollection, there were two or three Indian members on the board, one of whom was Khan Bahadur Mohammed Zakki, a retired government advocate from Gorakhpur. The other one was Jagan Prasad Rawat. The interview went off well, although there were a couple of amusing moments during the interaction with the interview board.

To cut a long story short, RNK managed to get into the IP when the results were declared in March 1940. By his own admission, Kao was lucky to get into the IP that year. 'I managed to get in just by the skin of my teeth because initially from UP, they were going to take only two candidates. Later, it was discovered that because of the war [Second World War], not enough recruits for the IP were available in India. So, they decided to take one more man and I managed to get in,' RNK noted years later.

The family was elated. For his mother, it was perhaps the greatest day in her largely joyless life after her husband had passed away when she was just 25. 'She had pinned all her hopes on me, and I had finally made my mark although in school, I had been rather an indifferent student. So, her joy knew no bounds, and I must mention that my younger brother was also transported with joy at the fact that I had finally made good,' Kao recalled.

Here, it is worth noting the role played by RNK's mother in moulding the two brothers, and RNK's bond with his younger brother. He credits his mother for motivating the two siblings to succeed in life since she, as a young widow, had nothing much to look forward to except to see her children do well in life. 'She exercised a strict vigilance over me and also enforced very strict discipline. She was not above chastising me physically on several occasions ... (yet) my mother was also the best mother that anyone could hope to have. She was doting and gave me unstinted love and made her twosome the centre of her existence. To this date, I recall her attitude and love, the innumerable nights when she kept awake fanning me in the hot, sultry weather of Baroda. Her ordeal had become more exact on account of the fact that I had frequent bouts of malaria and dysentery, which necessitated a strict diet and maintenance of a tight regimen,' Kao recalled years after she had passed away.

RNK also doted on his brother. His brother, Shyam Sunder Nath Kao, was born after their father had passed away. 'I should mention that my younger brother is six years junior to me. Initially, I had come to expect more or less complete monopoly of my mother's affection, more so after her widowhood. So, my baby brother appeared to me to be my rival for my mother's attention. This, of course, wore off as I grew older, and today, I think, that my brother and I are good friends and very close to each other. For this, the credit should go entirely to my brother,' RNK recalled.

In fact, the bond was so strong that in January 2002, when the younger brother had to be admitted to the ICU of Ram Manohar Lohia hospital, RNK was beside himself with worry. And despite his own reasonably good health, got himself admitted in the same hospital to be close to his brother. No one will know what went through RNK's mind that January in 2002 as his brother fought for his life in the ICU, almost wishing for his own death. It was as if RNK did not wish to contemplate a life without his brother. However, the fact is that Rameshwar Nath Kao passed away on 20 January 2002 before his brother did a few days later.

To get back to RNK's joining the IP, after doing the mandatory medical examination, RNK had to get his uniform, the mess kit, shoes, riding boots—everything that was necessary for daily use as an IP probationer—from designated shops in Lucknow. Kao described his state of mind in detail.

'Then came the excitement of having my uniform made before I joined the Police Training College at Moradabad. I remember that I had my khaki uniform made by a tailor from Lucknow cantonment. There was also a shoemaker, who made my riding boots and my polo boots in accordance to the specifications. Then I went to Anderson and Company in Lucknow, where I had a dinner jacket made. It was quite a new experiment because as a student, I never had the money to go to any first-class tailor, and Anderson, in those days, was still an English-run firm, and I still wear the trousers he made for me then. The material was beautiful.'

Duly kitted out, RNK arrived at the Police Training College in Moradabad and reported for duty on 7 April 1940. He was given a room in the Officers' Mess, which was actually a cavernous old building, dating back to the First World War. He had a large room with an attached bathroom allotted. A Gorkha, Jeep Bahadur, had accompanied RNK from Lucknow. Life appeared to be beautiful at that moment. RNK was also fortunate to have Dyan Swarup Sharma and Amarjit Kumar Das as his course mates, both known to him from his days in the hostel of Allahabad University.

Kao's first encounter with British Police officers was, however, far from cordial. Having excelled in English Literature and read romantic poems of Milton, Shelley, Keats and writings of Shakespeare, RNK's first close contact with the Britishers was a rude awakening. 'Who should I find in the police but people who appeared to me only semi-literate, very crude, rough and using swear words and generally arrogant in behaviour. In the beginning, this caused me a lot of distress,'

Kao recalled. Initially, the Britishers did not approve of RNK's insistence on remaining a teetotaller, but later they accepted him for what he was.

Interestingly, the conduct of the probationers in the mess, outside and even the way they behaved in the rooms, was under constant watch by the Principal, who seemed to have a number of informants. Kao realised this one evening in the mess after dinner when he was playing billiards. During the game, a discussion on the Indian National Movement, led by the Congress began. Suddenly, the Principal turned around and said, 'If you want to know anything about the National Movement led by the Congress, ask Kao, because he reads the *Hindustan Times*.'

*Hindustan Times*, it must be noted, was seen as a supporter of the Indian freedom movement, which was obviously noticed by the Principal. Police officers under the British were expected to only read *The Statesman* from Delhi or get *The Pioneer* from Lucknow. 'This was an eye-opener for me. Those were difficult days during the War, and I had to be very careful and watch my step. There were no unpleasant incidents as such, but one distinctly had the feeling of being kept under observation,' RNK noted.

Once in a while, Indian food was prepared in the mess and RNK remembered on one such occasion, a British officer asking him, 'Does this food taste as bad as it looks?'

All this was rather galling, Kao remembered. Indians could not play Indian music on the radio in the mess. Early during his stay in Moradabad, RNK imbibed a lot of knowledge about various drinks, liquor and wines, because he was designated to work as the 'C' (or Cellar) Officer for nearly six months. He had to keep individual accounts of the liquor consumed by various people. He noted that that was, in itself, quite an interesting education.

'Frequently, we had mess nights, when a number of army officers and officers of the IP from neighbouring districts were invited. Those were very boring occasions for me, because we were the junior-most people and we could not leave the mess until the senior guests had departed, and quite often it would be nearly 3 AM by the time we used to get back to our rooms. Then we had to be up again by 5 AM to attend the parade. That really was quite tiring, and a lot of drinking used to go on,' Kao recalled.

Riding was an integral part of Police Training College. RNK had, in fact, acquired a horse within a week of his arrival at Moradabad. He remembered having bought it from a Police officer called Thorat, who was a Deputy Superintendent under training from the state of Gwalior. RNK says, 'I think his brother later became a General in the Army (Lt General P.P. Thorat, who retired as Eastern Army Commander in the early 1960s). This particular Thorat later joined the Maharashtra Police from Gwalior, and I remember the last time I met him was when he was a Deputy Commissioner of Police in Bombay.'

RNK kept the horse for seven years and became quite proficient in riding, although he had one fall that almost resulted in a serious injury. Gradually, the cost of maintaining the horse went up, and Kao could no longer afford to keep it.

Weeks and months went by in Moradabad. Occasionally, the officers used to be invited by the Nawab of Rampur to the neighbouring town of Rampur, about 80 miles from Moradabad. These used to be quite memorable events as they were feasted and dined by the Nawab in his palace. The Nawab also screened private cinema shows. On one occasion, the famous movie *Gone with the Wind* was screened.

The Principal's wife, Mrs Field, used to pay great attention to the training of Indian officers in acquiring social graces. 'It seemed to me that one of the chief objects of the kind of life, which was imposed on us at the Officer's Mess, was to convert us into some kind of brown-snobs. It was strange that a strict caste system was enforced there and anyone who was not a member of the Secretary of State Services or a Commissioned Officer in the Defence Services was not permitted to enter the mess. In the beginning, this seemed very strange to me, because many of my friends from the university days or, at least, a few of them who had also taken the competitive examination along with me and had not qualified for the IP had got into the Provincial Police Services. They were being trained along with the IP officers; they attended the same classes and outdoor work, and some of them were, in fact, better than the IP officers, and, yet, while they might, sort of, visit us once in a while in our room in the mess, they could never be allowed to enter the dining hall and the Officer's Mess as such,' RNK noted.

Even in their day-to-day conversation, Indian officers were encouraged to affect a contemptuous attitude towards the average Indian. In this, they were encouraged to assiduously reflect the views and opinions of their British colleagues, Kao remembered. The training in Moradabad continued until the end of 1940, and for practical district training, during the months of January and February of 1941, RNK was posted to Khiri, which was the headquarters of the Lakhimpur Khiri district. Thereafter, RNK got posted to various districts, spending nearly seven years in the United Provinces.

Even as he was contemplating the future and his career in the IP, after spending six–seven years in service, Kao was deputed to the Directorate of Intelligence Bureau in 1947.

Founded as an ad hoc organisation in the late 19th century by a British civil servant working with the East India Company, the Intelligence Bureau (IB) was formally organised in 1920, modelled after the British Security Service, MI5. Throughout India's freedom struggle during the first 47 years of the 20th century, the IB became an indispensable arm of the repressive British regime, keeping tabs on Indian freedom fighters and political leaders. Post-Independence, however, the IB's mandate expanded to keep a watch on India's adversaries and its neighbours. Collection of intelligence from India's border areas became an important function of the IB in the post-Second World War years.

T.G. Sanjeevi Pillai, IB's first India Director between 1947 and 1950, consciously tried to change the job profile and philosophy of the organisation by inducting more Hindu officers. In fact, according to M.K. Narayanan, who served as the IB Chief in the late 1980s, and later as National Security Adviser, RNK had the distinction of being the first

Hindu officer to join the IB.[1] Under the British, the IB used to be dominated by white British officers and a smattering of Muslims.

As he joined the IB, Kao started working closely with Bhola Nath Mullik, then Pillai's deputy and later IB's longest serving director from July 1950 to October 1964. When he took over as IB's second director, Mullik made Kao in-charge of the security of the prime minister. As a Deputy Director in the IB, apart from looking after the security detail of Prime Minister Nehru, Kao was also entrusted with overseeing the security arrangements of visiting foreign dignitaries.

There is an incident worth recalling. In 1950, England's Queen Elizabeth was on a visit to India. Kao was heading the security and travel arrangements of the British Monarch. In Bombay, the Queen was wading through a huge crowd which was kept in control by the police. Kao was keeping a hawk's eye on the surroundings when he noticed something being hurled at the queen. Instinctively, Kao caught the package hurled towards the Queen, which turned out to be a flower bouquet, and not a bomb as Kao suspected. Noticing his quick reaction, the Queen apparently drolly remarked 'good cricket'.[2] Apocryphal or not, this incident shows that Kao had an alert mind and presence.

It was only natural that Nehru would send the then 37-year-old RNK to be a special investigator to enquire into

---

[1] https://koausa.org/rnkao/gentleman.html

[2] https://www.independent.co.uk/news/obituaries/r-n-kao-9204116.html

the crash of an Air India aircraft, named Kashmir Princess, off the coast of Indonesia on 11 April 1955.

Prime Minister Nehru had conceived of an Afro-Asia conference to be hosted by Indonesia at Bandung. It was scheduled to be held between 18 and 24 April 1955. The Air India International Super Constellation plane was chartered by the Chinese Government to carry its delegates for the inaugural conference.

It had left Bombay on 10 April and reached Hong Kong around noon, local time, the next day after a refuelling halt at Calcutta, and a change of crew at Bangkok. The plan was to carry the Chinese delegation from Hong Kong to Jakarta. In the first trip, the advance Chinese party consisted of eight Chinese officials, two Polish journalists and one North Vietnamese official besides five crew members. The Kashmir Princess took off from Kai Tak airport, Hong Kong, on 11 April 1955 around 1:30 local time. It was supposed to land at Jakarta that evening.[3]

However, after a five-hour journey, it crashed near Indonesia's Natuna islands. All 11 passengers and five of the eight crew members died in the crash. Three crew members survived, and swam to an isolated island, and were saved by local fishermen. These crewmen, later, revealed that they had heard murmurs of sabotage at Hong Kong. They revealed that no security drill or thorough check was carried out during the halt at Hong Kong and many people had access to the plane. As

---

[3] From the book by the then Indian Defence Attache in Indonesia, Col A.K. Mitra (retd), *Disaster in the Air: The crash of the Kashmir Princess 1955* (New Delhi: Reliance Publishing House, 2017).

it transpired, anticipating (wrongly as it turned out) Chinese Premier Zhou Enlai's presence on the plane, a Formosa (now Taiwan) Intelligence operative, masquerading as an aeroplane technician, had planted a bomb on the aircraft during the halt at Hong Kong. The intent was clearly to assassinate the Chinese Premier.

Shaken by this close shave, Zhou Enlai requested Prime Minister Nehru for Indian assistance in the probe. Britain too joined the enquiry since Hong Kong was then a British territory. On the advice of the then IB Chief, B.N. Mullik, Nehru deputed RNK to represent India in the trilateral probe.

Prime Minister Nehru, an itinerant politician and statesman, travelled the world frequently. RNK invariably accompanied him on every tour, be it at home or abroad, after he returned from the Kashmir Princess investigation. The wide exposure to high dignitaries, top officials and the intricate discussions and negotiations, stood RNK in good stead in later years when he founded the R&AW. Working closely with India's longest serving prime minister brought RNK in contact with many intelligence chiefs during his travels abroad. He was also noticed by Nehru for his quiet efficiency and meticulousness. This was to stand him in good stead, as RNK rose in hierarchy and started occupying central position in the secretive world of intelligence and espionage.

# THREE

# Ramji: The Gentle Giant

'He was a noble man!' This was how Malini Kao, the frail 99-year-old widow of Rameshwar Nath Kao, described her husband as she sat at the dining table in the Kao household in July 2019. Even though largely confined to her bedroom and most of her faculties failing her, she seemed energised when she was told that a book on RNK was at a planning stage, and that the author wanted to meet her. 'He had an outstanding career,' Malini Kao added as an afterthought. Straining to remember their life together (they were married for 60 years), she described RNK as a loyal and gentle man, who never thought ill of anybody.

RNK, a devout Hindu, was deeply spiritual and practiced meditation and puja every day. A devoted family man, RNK and Malini Kao had stayed with RNK's younger brother and his wife as a joint family under one roof all their life. In the Kashmiri Pandit community, the brothers were known as

'Ram-Lakshman *ki jodi*' (pair) because of their close bond. Their bungalow in Vasant Vihar is, in fact, aptly named Saketa (Ayodhya), the abode of Prabhu Ramchandra. RNK had an unparalleled sense of duty, which he fulfilled as the family's patriarch.

Their daughter Achala Kao, now Achala Kaul, remembers RNK as a man with strong convictions about right and wrong. 'He never pontificated and always led by example. He used to say, '*nasihat mat do, namuna ban jao.*' (Don't advise, set an example for others to follow.) That was the essence of the man,' Achala says, her face glowing with justifiable pride.

Malini Kao narrated the incident when the couple had met Ma Anandamayi. RNK greeted her with a *pranam*, when she asked, '*Kya naam hai tumahara?*' (What's your name?) When he told her that his name is Ramji, the saint said, '*Jas naam thata gun.*' (The man has attributes that go with the name.) In the Hindu religion and mythology, Ram is considered an epitome of duty and principle. The Saint apparently saw similar characteristics in RNK. He was well versed in the Gita and the Ramayana.

A very disciplined and punctual man, RNK disliked sloppiness. His routine was set. Breakfast at 9 AM, lunch at 1:30 PM and dinner at 9 PM. 'When he used to ask us to be ready by 8, we made sure that we were ready by 5 to 8,' Achala recalls. A teetotaller and vegetarian, RNK nevertheless was an extremely gracious host and served alcohol to his guests. Malini Kao was a good cook and enjoyed entertaining people. Meticulous to the core, he always wore three-piece suits during winters and white, khadi bush shirts in summer months. He had immaculate taste and was particular about dress and manners.

Hormis Tharakan, who headed the R&AW between 2005 and 2007, has a memory of his last meeting with RNK. 'I met him for the last time in the winter of 1998 just before I left Delhi on transfer. When Molly, my wife and I reached Vasant Vihar, Mr Kao, wearing a perfectly-stitched pinstripe suit and Mrs Kao, with a smiling face as always were waiting in the drawing room to receive us. Caught up in the evening Delhi traffic, we were about 15 minutes late. As I expected, Mr Kao remarked on the delay with some displeasure. He was always a stickler for time. But thereafter, he got fully involved in hospitality. Although he had only a soft drink, he would pour me nothing but Scotch (that too, Black Label). Though I said I would get the second drink myself, he did not agree. He got up with some difficulty, and poured another drink for me.'

The couple were mentors to two generations of R&AW sleuths. Vikram Sood, who joined the agency in 1972 and rose to become its Chief in 2001, says, 'The impression I formed about RNK in the first meeting was only reinforced over the years; he was a father figure who led by example.'

This sentiment is echoed across the board—by his colleagues, by his subordinates and by the people who interacted with him professionally. Sankaran Nair who succeeded RNK in 1977 as the second Chief of the department—albeit briefly—had this to say about Kao, 'Ramji ... a person of high intellect, a true Hindu and a man who will not harm his worst enemy. Once I found one of our ex-colleagues, who had retired, waiting to see him for some favour. I queried Ramji why he was willing to help this man who had been spreading false rumours about him. His reply was that rumours would not harm him, but any assistance provided to our ex-colleague would help him.'

The friendship and professional collaboration between Nair and RNK is legendary in the secretive world of foreign intelligence. Their contribution in building an organisation from scratch is a rare success story in post-Independence India. RNK and Nair were different like day and night, but their bond went beyond their individual personalities. And RNK's saintly demeanour amused and irritated his friends, such as Nair, no end. As he remarked to RNK with reference to the above cited incident, 'Ramji, you should be sitting in a cave in the Himalayas contemplating your navel. But don't forget to store scotch in the cave for my occasional visits!'[1]

But RNK was not all about official work alone. He had an artistic bent of mind—a man who loved to sculpt and someone who had an eye for beauty. He worked with wood, clay and stone. He was a man with a strong sense of smell and loved fragrant flowers. 'In our house, fresh flowers used to be changed twice a day,' Achala fondly recalls.

In his post-retirement years, RNK pursued his hobby of sculpting more vigorously and frequented the Garhi village in Delhi. He was a great patron of young artists and encouraged them, since RNK felt that artists always struggle for survival.

---

[1] K. Sankaran Nair, *Inside IB and RAW: The Rolling Stone that Gathered Moss* (New Delhi: Manas Publications, 2019).

During his frequent visits to Garhi, he came across a young artist named Mohammad Sadiq and worked with him. Today Sadiq is settled in London but still keeps in touch with the family. 'We always receive Diwali greetings from him every year,' Achala says.

RNK had great love for animals. Very early in his police career, RNK had developed a love for horses. Dogs were always a part of the household. Later in life, when all the pet dogs died one after the other, RNK would make sure stray dogs in the locality were fed and sheltered properly. Achala remembers, 'If it was raining and RNK noticed a stray trying to find shelter, he would tell the domestic help, "*woh phatak ko khol doh, unhe andar rahne doh*"' (Open the gate. Let them stay inside.)

'He was, of course, very protective about me and he was very discreet about keeping a watch on me. Every morning, he would gently and casually ask, 'So what's your programme?' I didn't realise back then, but there was always someone around discreetly keeping an eye on me. I remember, once I had gone to watch a movie in the old Odeon theatre with a friend when electricity failed. There were a very few people in the hall. We were waiting for the lights to come back when a man came and said, "Madam, *yeh Bijli aane mein do-tin ghante lag jayenge. Aap chale jayiye.*" (It will take two–three hours for electricity to be restored. You should better leave.) Much later, I realised that he must have been the minder sent by Daddy,' Achala recalls.

As the Kao brothers got on in age, Anil Kaul, a corporate professional who worked in Mumbai, decided to shift with them in Delhi. There, during RNK's later years, Anil experienced the awe in which RNK was held.

'After Mr Kao's demise, once I was out for my usual walk in Vasant Vihar when an elderly gentleman taking a stroll with his wife stopped me and asked, "Are you Kao's son-in-law?" When I nodded yes, he remarked, "What a man! What achievements. *Faristha tha.*" (He was an angel.) The gentleman just wouldn't stop praising Mr Kao. Just then, his wife butted in and addressing me she said, "Do you know, even my husband was a Governor?" The moment she said that, the old man flared up and said, "*Kya baat karti ho! Kahan Kao Sahib, kahan mein!*" (What are you saying? Look at Kao Sahib's stature and look at mine!) On another occasion, I was passing by the Senior Citizens Club in our locality when an elderly man stopped me and after confirming I was Mr Kao's son-in-law, broke down, resting his head on my chest and sobbing away. I didn't know how to react. I just stood there, dumbfounded. That is the kind of respect and veneration he commanded,' Anil Kaul said.

There are many other happier memories Kaul has about RNK—the avuncular patriarch of the house—such as the way he treated the domestic help, the subordinate staff and even strangers who asked for assistance.

Once, on a flight from Bombay to Delhi, Kaul had spotted Field Marshal Sam Manekshaw. He went up to him and introduced himself as RNK's son-in-law. Sam, as Mankeshaw was generally known, broke into a genuine smile and exclaimed, 'Ramji, my good friend! How is he? Son-in-law, uh? Sit, sit. Tell me, how's Malini? How are they keeping?'

Manekshaw was beside himself just at the mention RNK's name. 'For the next 15 minutes, he made me sit next to him and chatted about their times together,' Kaul remembers. Sam and RNK, besides others, were the pivotal figures in India's 1971 campaign to liberate East Pakistan. They not only had genuine professional partnership but had developed a close personal bond as well.

On another occasion, Kaul accompanied RNK to a big function to honour the Dalai Lama. It was organised at the convention centre of The Ashok Hotel in Delhi. More than 1,500 people attended the event. As was his wont, RNK had preferred to sit many rows away from the front in an aisle seat. As the Dalai Lama arrived, everyone in the hall stood up. As he made his way to the stage, the Dalai Lama was responding to greetings from people on either side of the passage, when he suddenly spotted RNK. 'The moment he recognised Mr Kao, the Dalai Lama's face broke into a big, broad smile. He stopped, clasped Mr Kao's hands with both of his hands and said, "Kao! How are you, my friend?" The Dalai Lama was beside himself with sheer joy. Mr Kao, on the other hand, was embarrassed by the public recognition. Fortunately, the organisers gently took the Dalai Lama forward,' Kaul remembers vividly.

Even foreign interlocutors had only words of praise for RNK. B. Raman, another former R&AW officer, quotes a French spy Chief, Count Alexandre de Marenches, who included RNK as one of the five great intelligence chiefs of the 1970s. De Marenches had remarked, 'What a fascinating mix of physical and mental elegance! What accomplishments!

What friendships! And yet, so shy of talking about himself, his accomplishments and his friends.'

It was this loyalty, a sense of purpose and innate shyness that prevented RNK from writing his memoirs or give interviews. Despite being active till the end, for 18 years after giving up his formal positions in the government, RNK did not speak at any public function, refrained from interacting with the media or write his autobiography. And, he had so much to share and reveal! After all, here was a man who played a major part in helping the Bengalis of East Pakistan create a new nation, secured the merger of Sikkim into the Indian dominion and build the R&AW into a formidable outfit, comparable to the best in the world. In this context, one incident comes easily to mind.

In 1996, several functions were held in Delhi to commemorate the 25th anniversary of the birth of Bangladesh, which was attended by many who were associated with it in one way or the other. At one such meeting, a Bangladeshi citizen, familiar with Delhi's who's who, noticed a handsome, impeccably dressed man sitting at the back of the room, as if trying to make himself inconspicuous. The Bangladeshi realised it was RNK. So, he went up to him and said, 'Sir you should have been sitting at the centre of the dais. You are the man who made 1971 possible.' Embarrassed at being spotted, RNK replied, 'I did nothing. They deserve all the praise.' After that, he quietly left the hall.

Many others have similar stories about his simplicity, his obsession with keeping a low profile and polite behaviour even at the peak of his power and influence. Vappala Balachandran, an IPS officer of 1959 batch, who joined the R&AW in 1976 after spending 17 years in Maharashtra Police, worked closely with RNK in his post-1977 years. After his retirement in 1996, Balachandran has been a prolific commentator on national security affairs. Speaking to me at his elegant flat in Mumbai, Bala, now in his early eighties, recalls an incident at an IB conference in December 1975. In August of that year, Bangladesh's founding father, Sheikh Mujibur Rahman, and nearly 40 members of his family were massacred by disgruntled Bangladeshi Army officials, sending shock waves across the subcontinent. There were also whispers about the R&AW's failure to prevent the carnage. Middle-level police officials from all states in the country were attending the DIG-CID conference in Delhi. RNK was one of the speakers in the three-day meeting. After RNK's opening remarks, a DIG from Madhya Pradesh, perhaps wanting to confirm the alleged failure of R&AW in not being able to save Mujibur Rahman, asked, what seemed an impertinent question to the audience. As Balachandran remembers, 'DIG Qureshi from MP asked a particularly loaded question as to why our external intelligence was caught napping about the Bangladesh coup. As we all squirmed in our seats at the expected explosion from RNK, who was at the peak of his power and influence, all that he was willing to say in his inimitable style was, "I can assure you that we were not surprised at the developments." There was no attempt to browbeat the questioner on the basis of his seniority or to show off his foreknowledge—instead a factual understatement was provided, which was the hallmark of the traditionalist, British-trained spy Chief.'

Vikram Sood, amongst the first to join R&AW from allied services (he came from the Indian Postal Service), and who rose to become one of its most respected Chiefs in the early 2000s, remembers RNK to be suave, extremely polite and very stylish right after his first encounter with the legend. 'After I was told by my service that I have been shortlisted to be deputed to a new organisation (in those days, no one spoke of the R&AW, as it was all very secretive), I was interviewed by Mr Sankaran Nair followed by Mr Kao. Even after all these years, I remember being dumbfounded in Mr Kao's presence, although the interaction was brief. He was not looking for knowledge or cunningness from me. There were no tricky questions either. All that Mr Kao and Mr Nair were doing was to size me up. Of course, they asked me if I was prepared to spend my life in this organisation. That was easy. I had no intention to spend the rest of my career in the postal service.'

Sood, who has recently authored an important book on the art and craft of intelligence, and is now something of an elder statesman for the outfit, says, 'RNK inculcated a habit for precision and meticulousness in our functioning. We could not make a mistake in our report. We could not be anything but be meticulous in our reporting. Each word had to be weighed. Sometimes, your report would come back marked with a tick and a remark, 'off'. *Aap raat bhar sochte rah jaate, kaise miss ho gaya.* (You would think the entire night, how did you miss that.) That is the kind of precision he wanted in your communication; he led by example. He did not shout even if he wanted to be stern with someone. He was very particular about conducting meetings. RNK did not like anyone speaking out of turn or anyone interrupting when a conversation was on.'

Sood says that he will remember his last meeting with RNK forever. 'We used to have an annual get together where serving and retired officers used to come together for an evening. That particular day in 2001, I got delayed in official meetings since there was an alarm—false as it turned out—about terrorists having entered the Doordarshan headquarters. As I reached the headquarters, almost 90 minutes late, Mr Kao spotted me. "Okay good, now that you have come, I can go." Embarrassed, I said, "You could have left any time, Sir." "How can I go before the Chief has come?" Kao remarked. That was the last I saw him. I still have a picture, a rarity, from that meeting,' Sood reminiscences as he looks back at the remarkable man who shaped R&AW's destiny.

That was quintessential Kao. A private man, who shunned the limelight, hated to be photographed and preferred to work behind the scenes, even in his personal life.

# The Kashmir Princess Investigation

April 1955 was considered to be a turning point in RNK's career, when he was assigned a case that gave him a big boost and proved to be, in his own words, an 'important landmark'. The case had international ramifications and took RNK to five different countries and gave him an exposure to different cultures, policing approaches and detective works.

This was his first major assignment abroad—one on which RNK spent 6 months abroad. It presented him the opportunity of seeing new lands and meeting a number of foreign dignitaries, the most distinguished of whom was Zhao Enlai (Chou en-Lai, as spelt in those years), the Chinese Premier. RNK's duty took him to Singapore, Indonesia, the Philippines, Hong Kong and China. In his own words, 'This was my first exposure to South East Asia, which, by all accounts, is a fascinating world in itself. It is so close to us, yet about which general knowledge in India is poor.'[1]

The investigation was about the crash of an Air India aircraft named Kashmir Princess.

There is a back story to the entire incident. Prime Minister Nehru had conceived an Afro-Asia conference to be hosted in Indonesia at Bandung. It was scheduled to be held between 18 and 24 April 1955. The Air India International Super Constellation plane was chartered by the Chinese Government to carry its delegates for the inaugural conference, along with the Premier. Zhou Enlai's adversaries, looking for an opportunity to assassinate him, planted a bomb on the plane during its halt at Hong Kong. The plane crashed in South China Sea (see Chapter 2). RNK was deputed to represent India in the subsequent investigations.

According to RNK—he put in his own effort at piecing together the sequence of events—the plane took off with 8 crew members and 11 passengers from Hong Kong for Jakarta. About 5 hours after take-off, a muffled explosion was heard. At that time, the aeroplane was flying at about 18,000 feet over the sea. Soon after the explosion, smoke started entering the cabin and fire was detected in the starboard rig behind the third engine. The captain of the aircraft, Captain Jatar, decided to ditch the aeroplane and for this, the prescribed drill was quickly and methodically carried out. The descent was rapid, and its final stage was carried out under extremely difficult circumstances.

---

[1] R.N. Kao papers, serial No. 2, NMML, New Delhi.

The aeroplane fell into the sea, with the starboard hitting the water first and the nose sinking almost immediately. The aircraft was burned and destroyed as a result of the impact and out of the passengers and crew members, only three crew members survived. The survivors were flight navigator Pathak, aircraft mechanical engineer Karnik and co-pilot Dixit. The captain of the aircraft, Captain Jatar, who was one of the most experienced pilots of Air India international, died in his seat and, in fact, when the salvage operations took place later, his body was found in the captain's seat. The very first accounts received also confirmed that the airhostess, Miss Glori Asponson, had acted most heroically. She maintained her calm in that extremely trying conditions and, as was later confirmed after examining the dead body that was recovered, she issued lifebelts to every single passenger as well as member of the crew, before the aircraft actually hit the water.

It was clear, almost from the very beginning, that the aircraft, Kashmir Princess, had been the victim of sabotage. This incident assumed great importance as a number of countries were involved. The aircraft was Indian, but the passengers were all Chinese. It had taken off from Hong Kong and had crashed in Indonesian waters.

The Government of India was not only directly concerned with this case, because the aircraft was Indian, but also because at that time, in 1955, the British did not have any regular diplomatic connection with the Chinese. In keeping with these circumstances, the Government of India designated a big team from the Civil Aviation Department to be associated with all aspects of the investigation. K.M. Raha, who was then the Deputy Director General of the Civil Aviation Department, headed the team. His advisers were Col A.K. Mitra, who was India's military attaché in Jakarta at that time, and Y.R. Malhotra, Chief Inspector of Accidents, Civil Aviation Department in the Government of India.

Almost immediately after the accident, Chinese radio announced that the Chinese Government had information that the Kashmir Princess had been the victim of sabotage. The Chinese blamed KMT (Kaumingtang, Taiwanese Government) agents for the crime. In view of these implications, it was decided, with the approval of Prime Minister Nehru, that apart from the team sent by the Civil Aviation Department, an intelligence officer from India should be deputed to be associated with the investigation by the intelligence authorities concerned.

RNK was handpicked by the Director of Intelligence Bureau (DIB), Bhola Nath Mullik, for the crucial assignment. 'Later I understood that the Prime Minister had informed the British Prime Minister, Sir Anthony Eden, of my nomination. It was considered necessary because it was rightly believed that the main burden of the inquiry would have to be handled by the Hong Kong Police and if I were to play any useful role, I would have to work in very close liaison with them. Having got the necessary clearance from all the authorities concerned, I was given green signal by Shri Mullik and asked to proceed to Bombay on the first lap of my journey. Accordingly, I left Delhi on 20 April 1955 by air for Bombay,' Kao noted.

RNK had chosen Chandra Pal Singh, a deputy central intelligence officer, to accompany him because he had full trust in his 'loyalty and integrity'. Kao knew Chandrapal for a long time. Vishwanathan, an engineer from the Hindustan Aircraft Factory, joined the team in Bombay where RNK interviewed the three survivors of the crash, Air India's District Manager and Operations Manager in Hong Kong, who were visiting India in connection with the enquiry.

In his notes left at the NMML, Kao records in 1977, 'I have not maintained any detailed records of the investigation amongst my personal papers, but from the jottings in my diary and from memory, I recall that in these interviews in Bombay, amongst other things, I gathered the complete list of the flight crew, passengers, leaders, cleaners, etc.. In fact, everyone who had access to the Kashmir Princess in Hong Kong before its flight. The details of the freight, mail and baggage were also similarly gathered by me. Having done this on 22 April in the evening, I left Bombay by air reaching Singapore the following day in the morning.'[2] After halting at Singapore airport for a couple of hours and a short meeting with Raha, RNK and his team left for Jakarta en route to Bandung, where the first Afro-Asian conference was about to happen. Many stalwarts from across the two continents had gathered there, including Nehru, Sukarno and Zhou Enlai.

As he reached Bandung, RNK was directed to the conference hall where the session was on. K.F. Rustomji, then a Deputy Director in the Intelligence Bureau and in-charge of the prime minister's security detail, immediately took RNK to Prime Minister Nehru. Nehru, at whose insistence RNK was told to join the investigation, had also arranged for RNK to

---

[2] Ibid.

meet the Chinese Premier that very evening. RNK was with Zhou Enlai for over an hour and then retired for the night.

RNK made an interesting observation during his first meeting with Zhou Enlai. 'Though he was wearing one of those boiler suits, it was clear that the material was neither ordinary nor was the cut. In spite of the cloth's colour and rather loose trousers and loose sleeves, all the Chinese leaders at the time sported a look keeping in mind the Mao style. Zhou Enlai was an impressive figure. He had an interpreter all along. He was a Harvard-trained Chinese who spoke English well. Though Mr Zhou Enlai spoke only in Chinese, his knowledge of English was better than he would acknowledge. At this meeting, I was, for the first time, exposed to Chinese green tea and various small eatables like dried lychee and other titbits. What struck me was the formal rectangular arrangement of the sofa and chairs. Opposite to the chairs, there was a table with plenty of ashtrays, with spittoons also provided near each chair. That, I later realised, was a standard Chinese décor.'

During the meeting, Zhou Enlai came quickly to the point and asked RNK to give an up-to-date information about what he had learned from the survivors. Based on what Pathak and Karnik had told him, RNK described the details of the bomb, where it was placed and what effect it had on the plane's engines that led to the crash. As RNK was explaining the sequence of events, he offered to draw a sketch too and took his fountain pen out.

What happened next can be best described in RNK's own words. 'He agreed with this enthusiastically. I took out some paper from my briefcase, which I was carrying, and I had a fountain pen in my pocket. I unscrewed the cap. I did not have much experience of air travel. Before I realised what was happening, I got a lot of ink on my fingers that had leaked out of the fountain pen while flying from Bombay to Singapore, Singapore to Jakarta and Jakarta to Bandung. Hence, I got ink on my fingers and I looked at it and tried to take out some white blank paper from my briefcase to wipe my fingers. Mr Zhou Enlai, without a word, rose from the sofa and left the room. This puzzled me but within a few minutes, he came back accompanied by an attendant who was carrying what looked to me like neatly folded wet towels. As I had never been exposed to Chinese wet towels, I looked at him inquiringly. He motioned that I should wipe my fingers on them. I was most impressed by his courtesy in taking the trouble of getting up, going out of the room and getting those towels for me to wipe my fingers. This was only the first of many polite, generous gestures that Mr Zhou Enlai made during my meetings with him.' RNK remember Zhou as a man who spoke briefly but to the point. And also, candidly. At one point, he insisted that RNK should not inform the British authorities of anything that was shared with him. Zhou, however, told RNK to proceed to Hong Kong and then visit Canton, where further arrangements would be made for him to meet Zhou.

The Bandung conference, which RNK was coincidentally attending, gave him the first opportunity to observe international meetings, protocols and false egos at work. As he entered the main plenary hall, RNK was taken to Prime

Minister Nehru who briefly instructed him and moved on to meet others.

'This was my first presence at an international meet and I was impressed with the solemnity of the occasion and the gravity which seemed to hang in the air. At that time, China had not widely been accepted as a respectable member of the international comity of nations, and as we (India) were one of the few countries that had established diplomatic relations with China, Prime Minister Nehru had taken upon himself the responsibility of introducing Zhou Enlai on the world scene. Or, at least, so he thought. In later years, I learned that Zhou Enlai had mentioned to some reporter that he had not met anyone as arrogant as Jawaharlal Nehru and in support of his statement, he had said that it was incredibly presumptuous on the part of the Prime Minister of India to have introduced the Prime Minister of China on the world scene. Well, whatever Zhou's ego might have been, the fact of the matter is Nehru did help China to gain recognition in the international field. In fact, in that process, we (India) earned a lot of odium,' Kao observed.

RNK also had a couple of other interesting anecdotes to share from his first international conference. 'I have a distinct recollection that Mr Mohammed Ali of Bogra, who was the then Prime Minister of Pakistan, was also there. He had brought along with him his wife, and as the proceedings started, I realised that Mr Mohammed Ali seemed more intent on teaching his wife how to use a cine camera to cover the proceedings, rather than to take part in it,' Kao remarked.

He also observed the egoistical behaviour of President Gamal Abdel Nasser of Egypt, who had hitched a ride on the Indian plane with Prime Minister Nehru to and from Bandung. 'It was interesting how unconsciously—although, I do not know whether it was unconscious—I got the impression that President Nasser was keen to give the impression that he, as a political figure, was at least as tall as Jawaharlal Nehru. Nehru himself being much older than Nasser tended to take him under his wing and brought him along in the aircraft. An interesting point of protocol was that normally when VIPs travel by aircraft, when you arrive at the place, the most important VIP first sets out of the aircraft. Similarly, when you are departing, everyone else is supposed to board earlier than the most important VIP. When they were leaving Jakarta for Bandung, Nehru put his hand around Nasser's shoulders and encouraged him to board the plane, but he would not do so, because he was keen on going up the stairs at the last. Finally, they decided to go up together,' Kao noted.

The next day, RNK left for Jakarta after briefing the Indian Prime Minister about the meeting with the Chinese Premier. On 26 April, RNK got involved with Nehru's security in the Indonesian capital, although he was not part of the security detail. Again, according to RNK's own notes, he met Nehru, who repeated his detailed instructions about the manner in which RNK should conduct the enquiry at Hong Kong. 'This was somewhat different from the instructions which Mr Mullik had given to me before I left Delhi. He had said that from Jakarta I should return to Singapore and make my headquarters there. In the light of the revelations made to me by Mr Zhou Enlai and the instructions given by Pandit Jawaharlal Nehru, I had no alternative but to proceed from Jakarta to Hong Kong as quickly as possible,' Kao noted.

So Hong Kong it was. After a circuitous journey from Jakarta to Hong Kong via Manila and Brunei—since seats were not available on direct Jakarta-Hong Kong route because of the rush of returning Bandung delegates—Kao and his assistants, Chandrapal Singh and Vishwanathan, reached Hong Kong on 30 April 1955. In between, they had to experience several difficult moments since travelling and logistics was not as advanced as one now sees in the South East Asian countries.

When the Indian team reached Jakarta, they discovered to their horror that tickets on direct flights to Hong Kong were unavailable for weeks. After a lot of effort and some help from the Indian Embassy, the three managed to buy a ticket to Manila from Jakarta on Indonesia's Garuda Airways. RNK was assured that the three Indians would be put onto a connecting flight to Hong Kong immediately. They did reach Manila in the Philippines—after making an unscheduled stopover at a small airstrip, which RNK later learnt was in Brunei—only to discover that they had no onward connection to Hong Kong! Kao and his team were forced to spend 24 hours in Manila, bereft of any Filipino currency or local support, before catching a flight to Hong Kong the next day.

India's Commissioner (not High Commissioner) at Hong Kong had arranged for their accommodation at a hotel called Miramar in Kowloon. This hotel became RNK's permanent address for the next six months as the investigations began in right earnest. As he started to liaise with the Hong Kong Police, Kao realised that he needed to make a trip to mainland China to get more insights. Again, RNK noted that he had a great difficulty in reaching Peking (as Beijing was then known) because of the combination of bad weather and poor connectivity.

On reaching Peking, Kao met Zhou almost immediately. As he had noted in their first meeting, the Chinese Premier came to the point directly. He said the Chinese Government had specific information that the alleged incendiary bomb, given by the United States, came from Taiwan and was placed in the wing of the aircraft by a Koumintang agent. The Chinese even had the names of the people suspected to be involved in the conspiracy. Chou wanted RNK to give this information to the Hong Kong Police, only if the British gave an assurance that they would keep it to themselves and not pass it on to the Americans at this stage.

Chou also told RNK that his (Kao's) life was in danger in Hong Kong and that he should take adequate precautions. Kao was, of course, aware of the pitfalls. 'Being a foreigner, I was quite conspicuous. This was emphatically underlined to me on my first visit to Beijing, where at the preliminary meeting with Mr Zhou Enlai, in grave terms, it was pointed out to me that the Chinese Government had information that the KMT intelligence clique, as they called it, was planning to assassinate me. He warned me that I should take good care of myself, because their information had come from a very reliable source. While I thanked him, I said that being a foreigner in Hong Kong and living in a hotel which is manned entirely by the Chinese, there was little that I could do to protect myself,' Kao noted in his recollection.

At the same time, RNK requested the Chinese Premier to inform the Governor of Hong Kong about their apprehension and take any measures they deemed fit to protect him. The request was promptly met. On his return to Hong Kong, the Director of the Hong Kong Special Branch met RNK and said he was instructed to provide adequate security to him. Accordingly, a British Inspector would accompany RNK, who would drive him around in Hong Kong in an unmarked car throughout his stay.

'All this came in very handy, although I do not know how far they were effective in protecting me against any attack by the KMT agents about whom Mr Zhou Enlai had warned me. But it was certainly convenient to have a police car, even if it is unmarked, and a British inspector of police to accompany me whenever I went out of the hotel. The person earmarked for this duty was a young British inspector of the Hong Kong Police, whom we shall call Jones,' Kao remarked.

The Chinese would not, however, let RNK sleep in peace. At least twice, Hsiung, the Chinese investigator stationed in Hong Kong and working with RNK, warned him about the strong possibility of an assassination attempt. 'Considering that the reports that the Chinese Government had received about the manner in which the Kashmir Princess had been sabotaged had been proved uncannily accurate, which left me with some uncomfortable feeling as I did not fancy myself ending my career lying in some obscure lane in Hong Kong with a knife in my back. In due course, however, I got used to living with the danger,' RNK wrote.

RNK was, however, experienced enough to take his own precautions, such as not walking the streets at night, avoiding bylanes and being careful about what he ate and where he ate. He recalled that one amusing fallout of these precautions was that he had to carry all the investigation-related papers in a briefcase all the time in the absence of a strong box or a safe. 'The briefcase was my constant companion even when I went out in the evenings for parties or any other social engagement, and, in due course, this became the subject of some amusement amongst my acquaintances, who referred to my briefcase as my darling, from whom I never could afford to be separated. In the hotel too I never lost sight of this briefcase. If I went to the bathroom, I took it with me and at night, I kept it under the mattress of my bed. I was able to relax some of these precautions a few months later when Rajan, the stenographer from Delhi, was sent to help me, because then it was often impossible for me to arrange for him to stand guard over these papers while I went out for some appointments,' RNK recalls.

As for the investigation itself, RNK was acutely conscious of the fact that this case had political overtones right from the beginning. His task was to ensure triangular liaison between India, China and the British. The Chinese were naturally quite agitated about the death of their nationals. 'They were also suspicious about the motive of the British, and, in this context, they also felt that some of the statements issued by the British Government in Hong Kong had overtones of the Cold

War. In this atmosphere, the Government of India generally, and Pandit Nehru personally, tried to act as a bridge between the English and the Chinese. This point was made by Pandit Nehru in his talks with Zhou Enlai in Bandung. In fact, Prime Minister Nehru then went on to reassure the Chinese Premier about the role of the Indonesian Government, who appeared to be sensitive and did not like being pushed into an inquiry,' Kao noted. In Bandung, Prime Minister Nehru also made a point to mention RNK's exact role to the Chinese Premier and told him that the Indian officer would succeed only if the Hong Kong Police as well as the Chinese authorities cooperated wholeheartedly.

However, RNK also faced a typical Indian turf war even before he formally joined the probe. The officer of the Civil Aviation Department, K.M. Raha, was unhappy that an engineer from his department was part of RNK's team. So was Col A.K. Mitra, the India's military attaché to Indonesia. Both thought that RNK and his team were getting more importance, and that their own position in the Indonesian Commission of Enquiry was being threatened. However, a direct intervention from Prime Minister Nehru, who wrote a long note to the Commonwealth Secretary explaining India's approach, finally convinced Messrs Raha and Mitra that RNK's team had nothing to do with them or their role.

To come back to the actual probe in Hong Kong, RNK went and met the Governor as soon as he returned from Beijing on 18 May 1955 and shared with him a list of suspects that the Chinese had prepared and also explained other relevant points from his meetings in Beijing. 'I stressed to the Governor that in order to retain the confidence of the Chinese, it was essential that immediate steps must be taken to ensure that the suspects identified by them did not run away. He agreed to have the matter examined by officers and arranged a meeting for me to meet them to discuss the plan of action,' Kao recalled.

His next meeting was with the Commissioner of Police, Maxwell, and the Director of Special Branch, Wilcox, and other British officers. Following the conference with the British officers, RNK went to meet Hsuing, the Chinese officer, and conveyed to him 'in general terms' that the British were taking immediate steps to secure the suspects. This three-way confabulation was in keeping with the instructions RNK had received from Prime Minister Nehru and DIB Mullik.

'Throughout these talks, I constantly kept in my mind the instructions given to me by Pandit Jawaharlal Nehru and repeated by Mr Mullik that I should try to retain the confidence of the British as well as the Chinese and do nothing that would later be challenged by either. An interesting part of the meetings I had with the Chinese in Beijing was that as far as they were concerned, the matter seemed to be dealt with only at the highest level. This was an evidence of the fact that they attached the greatest importance to the case. While in Beijing, I met only Premier Zhou Enlai and no one else. There were three meetings with him during my stay there. Hsiung, the police officer, was introduced to me only on the last day, when he quickly excused himself after the introduction and went out of the room,' RNK noted in his recollection.

The British were, however, less than truthful about the status of the suspects involved in the sabotage. RNK discovered this when he joined for dinner at Police Commissioner Maxwell's house a day after his return from Beijing, and after meeting the Governor and the police officers. Maxwell told RNK, without batting an eyelid, that the main criminal, Chou Chu (who had allegedly planted the bomb), had definitely managed to stow away in an American-owned civil transport company plane, which left Hong Kong Airport at 10 AM on 18 May, six hours before RNK arrived in Hong Kong and gave the names to the Governor!

RNK was shocked but recovered quickly to inform Hsiung about the escape of the main suspect. Commissioner Maxwell and others in Hong Kong, as if to console RNK, said had the information he had brought from Beijing been shared with them even eight hours earlier, the criminal would have been arrested. In his typically understated style, RNK wrote, 'This is a statement I would accept only with a pinch of salt.'

In fact, RNK felt he was caught in a pincer. The Hong Kong authorities pretended to take adequate interest in the case but constantly asked RNK to persuade the Chinese representative to part with more information, so that they could take proper action.

'The Commissioner of Police, whom I used to meet almost daily, and the Governor himself continued to go through the motion, urging me to ask Hsiung to give more information so that they could carry out determined action to liquidate the whole KMT terrorist gang in Hong

Kong. And they constantly begged for cooperation from the Chinese. In response to this, and perhaps in order to tire me out completely and exhaust my patience, in a typical Chinese style, Hsiung developed the habit of sending for me late at night or very early in the morning,' Kao noted. The Chinese representative was also less than forthcoming and adopted a coercive attitude towards RNK, remaining parsimonious about sharing information.

The British, during their informal interactions with Kao, confided in him that they were convinced about the sabotage angle but were not sure if the case would stand legal scrutiny in the court of law. They were dismayed that the Chinese, despite possessing full knowledge of the conspiracy and conspirators, shared the information too late and in small doses, which was inexplicable.

As days passed and investigations continued in fits and starts, Zhou Enlai arrived in Hong Kong towards the end of May 1955. After meeting the Governor, he also met RNK and said he was pleased with the way he (Kao) had gone about his task. Zhou, in fact, wrote a letter of appreciation about RNK to Prime Minister Nehru but continued to be sceptical about the intentions of the Hong Kong Police and the British authorities. Krishna Menon, who was then the leader of the Indian delegation to the UN but was arguably the second most-powerful man in India after Nehru, suggested to the Indian Prime Minister that DIB Mullik should visit Hong Kong to show India's seriousness in the investigations into the Kashmir Princess case, and also impress both the British and the Chinese.

Mullik arrived in Hong Kong in early June 1955, held separate meetings with the British and the Chinese sides, and, of course, took full briefing from RNK. 'In keeping with the policy decision by Pandit Jawaharlal Nehru regarding India's role in this investigation, Mr Mullik tried to bring about a better understanding between the Chinese, on the one hand, and the British authorities in Hong Kong, on the other. He was satisfied that the British were making genuine efforts to investigate the case, but the Chinese representative appeared to be unhappy because he felt that the British were being unduly secretive, and was agreeing to give to the Chinese information only about the specific case of sabotage and not any intelligence relating to the KMT espionage network, which had been operating in Hong Kong. Mullik was also good enough to appreciate my efforts to remain in touch constantly with both the sides and to keep the Chinese informed about the progress made by the British in the investigation of the case as far as possible,' RNK recalled.

Unexpectedly, within days of Mullik's return to India, Zhou made a formal complaint to Nehru alleging that Mullik was 'unduly partial' to the British in the investigation of the Kashmir Princess case. A distressed Nehru sent for Mullik and spoke to him about the allegation made by the Chinese Premier but dropped the matter once he realised that what Chou was referring to was untrue. Nehru then sent a letter to Chou emphatically denying any collusion between Mullik and the British. 'There was no question of any official of the Government of India, let alone Mr Mullik, either acting as an apologist of the Hong Kong Government or condoning any wrong action taken by them,' Nehru wrote.

Sensing the suspicion that the Chinese had with regard to the arrangement, Kao asked for a stenographer to be sent to assist him and be present in meetings with the Chinese representative. That's where Rajan—mentioned earlier as someone who would watch the briefcase when RNK went out—came in, and Chandrapal Singh went back to India.

Almost a week later, the Hong Kong Government announced publicly a reward of 100,000 Hong Kong dollars for anyone giving information that might lead to the arrest and conviction of the people who sabotaged the Kashmir Princess. Despite the reward and sincere investigation efforts by the Hong Kong Police, the probe seemed to have run into obstacles.

# Running into a Roadblock

By the middle of June 1955, it was clear to RNK that one of his objectives in joining the investigation on behalf of the Government of India was achieved. It was to ascertain whether the Kashmir Princess aircraft was a victim of sabotage or had suffered any mechanical failure. The Indonesian enquiry, meanwhile, had also been completed, and it had conclusively established that the crash had occurred because of a time bomb that was placed in the plane during its halt at Hong Kong.

The second task—that of liaising between Hsiung, the Chinese representative, and the Hong Kong authorities—was proving to be more and more difficult, since Hsiung was in no mood to be open with RNK. In the first fortnight or so, Hsiung did share ample intelligence and information but later he cooled off. The initial information was of three kinds:

1.  The first one relating directly to the sabotage.

2.   The second one relating to the KMT intelligence set up in Hong Kong, which was supposed to be behind the sabotage.

The third one containing allegations against some officers of the Special Branch of Hong Kong Police.

Kao observed, 'On the basis of the information given by the Chinese regarding the secret KMT intelligence organisation, the Hong Kong police raided various addresses and arrested a total of 25 people. From the statements made by some of them and the documents recovered from their possession, it was clear that the large KMT secret intelligence organisation had been functioning from Hong Kong. The enquiries in this regard were pursued energetically by the Hong Kong police and they were helped by some experts who had come from England.' However, it was one thing to uncover the KMT intelligence ring and quite another to link the organisation to the sabotage of Kashmir Princess. The Hong Kong Police felt that while the arrest was welcome, it was not really leading to any progress in the investigation of the crash of the Kashmir Princess, and so they specifically appointed officers to unravel the conspiracy of sabotage and tracing Chou Chu, the main accused.

Meanwhile, the Hong Kong authorities were quite convinced that they had no further use of Hsiung. He had requested RNK for copies of detailed interrogation and progress reports about the investigation. The Hong Kong Police did not agree to this. RNK felt it was quite possible that the Hong Kong authorities resented some of the allegations made by the Chinese regarding the secret KMT loyalties of some of their officers. In fact, they appeared to be keen on Hsiung leaving Hong Kong as soon as possible. This was, by turn, expressed in clear words during the second week of June by almost everyone with whom RNK was dealing with— the Governor, the Commissioner of Police, the Director of Special Branch and an officer of the Security Service, who had come down from London.

In the face of such a rigid attitude, there was little that RNK could do by way of liaison between the Chinese officer and the Hong Kong authorities. Privately, RNK was told that it would be difficult for them to give any information to the Chinese. RNK had, thus, reached a dead end in this matter.

'All these developments had led me to believe that my position at that time in Hong Kong will become increasingly difficult and the useful work that I could do, either for my own government or as liaison between the Chinese and the Hong Kong authorities, had been reduced to the minimum,' Kao noted.

RNK, being very perceptive and sharp, realised that the British wanted his proximity to the Chinese or, at least, have access to the top leadership, which could be exploited to get a better understanding of the Chinese thinking. 'The British were keen to get a better idea of the Chinese policy towards Indo-China, Burma, Siam (Thailand) Formosa and South Korea. They were also keen to get my opinion or through me, the Chinese view about their relations with the Russians, the extent of Russian aid to China and the behaviour of Russians in their dealing with Beijing. A crucial question that was engaging their attention was whether the summit talks that were then to be held in Geneva would be attended by the Chinese. And above all, they were keen to know about the Chinese government's policy towards overseas Chinese communities,' RNK wrote.

So even as the Hong Kong Police pursued the investigation at its own pace, RNK got more than adequate hints that he was no longer welcome in the island territory. And yet, his personal rapport with some of the important officers in the department meant that they kept giving RNK crucial inputs. On 20 June 1955, Hong Kong Special Branch Director, Willcox, revealed to RNK that the main accused Chou Chu's roommate named Chow Si Hok—who had been arrested earlier but was released due to lack of evidence—reappeared before the police. He was hoping to qualify for the reward of 100,000 Hong Kong dollar announced by the administration and narrated the sequence of events as they had happened a day before the Kashmir Princess was sabotaged.

Apparently, Chow Si Hok told the police that on 30 April, Chou Chu came to their room late at night, puffed a few drags of heroin and revealed how he had carried out the sabotage of Kashmir Princess, tempted by a promise of a handsome reward. According to Chow Si Hok, Chou Chu had been given a readymade bomb in the Movieland Hotel on 10 April, a day prior to the crash of the aircraft. Next morning, on 11 April, according to Chou Chu's statement to Chow Si Hok, he was taken by a KMT agent in a car and dropped off at the gate of the airport. Then, while cleaning the plane, he pushed the bomb in the cavity above the right wheel.

Two days later, when the news of the crash of the Kashmir Princess was all over the place, Chou Chu went to the KMT agent, who he was in touch with, to claim the reward. He was rebuffed by the KMT officer who said Zhou Enlai was not on the plane that crashed and, therefore, he would not get any money! A frustrated Chou Chu spilled the beans on earlier KMT attempts to assassinate Zhou Enlai too.

According to that confession, the plan was to apparently assassinate Zhou Enlai the previous year while the Chinese Premier was on his way back from Geneva via Hong Kong. Later, the KMT agents decided to assassinate Kuo Mo Ju, who went to India as the Head of Chinese delegation for the Asia Conference. However, when they heard that Zhou Enlai would be going to Bandung via Hong Kong, the plans were changed, and the conspiracy to sabotage the plane was hatched.

Meanwhile, the Director of Hong Kong Special Branch handed over to RNK a note to be passed on to the Chinese representative. The particular memorandum, RNK noted in his recollection, objected to the request for copies of the investigations be given to the Chinese, pointing out that it was not a British practice to share the findings of the investigations with another party. The same memorandum also noted that the Hong Kong Police had carefully followed up all the inputs given by the Chinese authorities about the main suspect Chou Chu, but their enquiries had revealed that there was insufficient corroborative evidence to prosecute Chou Chu and get a conviction in a court of law. The Chinese were not convinced. They were unable to understand the legal reasons behind the reluctance of the Hong Kong Police to pursue the case to its logical conclusion.

Meanwhile, Michael Hanley (later Sir Michael Hanley), the Hong Kong Representative of the British Security Service, more popularly known as the MI5, confided to RNK that the British authorities expected him to leave Hong Kong as soon as possible. 'I took Hanley's observations as a broad hint that if I stayed any longer, my position would become embarrassing,' RNK noted. Incidentally, Michael Hanley went on to become the head of MI5 between 1972 and 1978.

As a result of these developments, RNK was immediately asked to be withdrawn to India. Delhi, after careful consideration, however rejected the request. 'I understand that this matter was considered carefully by Mr S.N. Dutt of our Ministry of External Affairs, but it was felt that for political reasons and to avoid misunderstanding with the Chinese…, it had been decided that I should stay on in Hong Kong,' Kao wrote.

Throughout July 1955, however, RNK was repeatedly made to feel unwanted in Hong Kong. The Hong Kong Police were unwilling to share any meaningful information, and the Governor was reluctant to meet him. RNK felt the evident cold treatment of the Hong Kong authorities because of political reasons. 'In a meeting with me on the 11th July, apart from talking about other points, Mr Wilcox, the Director of the Special Branch, made an interesting observation. He repeated that there had been no further developments about the efforts to get Chou Chu back from Formosa (Taiwan). Then, he went on to observe that he thought that, in some respect, Chou Chu's return to Hong Kong at that stage might be a source of embarrassment to the Hong Kong Government rather than anything else,' RNK noted.

RNK went on to add that the case was becoming a political football. 'By then, we were in the beginning of August (1955) and my ding-dong negotiations with the Hong Kong officials, on the one hand, and my attempt, on the other hand, to maintain the link between them and the Chinese proceeded at a desultory place. At this stage, Mr Maxwell, the Commissioner of Police, appeared to be becoming more difficult and somewhat impatient,' RNK noted. Maxwell, according to Kao, was particularly disturbed about Prime Minister Nehru's statement in the Indian Parliament giving credit to the Chinese for giving a definite lead to the Hong Kong Police. Maxwell complained to RNK that despite their sincere attempts at investigating the case, Nehru had not acknowledged their contribution. However, RNK remembers reminding Maxwell that the Chinese had indeed given the name of the main suspect to the Hong Kong Police, so the Indian prime minister was not wrong in his contention.

Amidst all this, Zhou Enlai summoned Hsiung to Beijing and also sent a word that RNK should reach the Chinese capital by 20 August. Within days, the attitude of the Hong Kong authorities towards RNK changed. They began to pretend a little more than they were doing earlier, by taking him fully into confidence and the Commissioner of Police as well as the Governor turned on the charm offensive to keep Kao in good humour! They suddenly offered to RNK access to notes prepared by the Hong Kong Police and said he should explain to the Chinese Government, when he would visit Beijing, their inability to prosecute the KMT intelligence suspect. 'I could not help recalling that during the previous six weeks or more, the Hong Kong Police had not associated me with the sabotage enquiry and that suddenly when they realised I was to go to Beijing, they wanted me to bail them out...,' RNK wrote.

In another awkward development, Hsiung wanted RNK to accompany him to Beijing instead of going back home alone. This was contrary to the instructions that RNK had received from Mullik who wanted him to proceed to the Chinese capital at least four-five days after Hsiung had reached there. Meanwhile, the authorities in Hong Kong were going all out to impress upon RNK the absolute necessity of impressing upon the Chinese the sincerity with which the Hong Kong Police had investigated the case so far. RNK had no desire to do their bidding but had sought clear directions from Delhi on what his stand should be when he met the Chinese Premier.

The final instructions came in the third week of August. The gist of the instructions was that RNK should stick to reporting what the Hong Kong Police had shared with him and not express any opinion of his own. 'The idea was that I should not express any definite opinion on the merits of the case,' RNK recorded. He notes that Mullik had told him very clearly why this stand had to be taken. 'Mr Mullik had pointed out to me that while the Chinese Government would naturally like the entire KMT intelligence set up in Hong Kong to be rounded up and prosecuted, India's interest was limited to the prosecution of the gang immediately responsible for sabotaging the Kashmir Princess,' RNK wrote. The DIB warned him against making any comments on whether it was possible for the Hong Kong authorities to collect further evidence to implicate other persons in this gang or not.

In the meantime, in keeping with their changed attitude, the Hong Kong authorities shared, in private, their report on the probe thus far with RNK. In the report shared by Willcox, the police were able to confirm that the key figure in the conspiracy was a man named Wu, who was, however, neither identified nor located. According to the report, however, Wu appeared to be a high-grade KMT agent who had enlisted the services of Chou Chu alias Chau Tse Ming alias Chau Kui as the main saboteur.

Interestingly, the report also mentioned that if the Hong Kong authorities had appointed a Commission of Enquiry instead of going for a straight police case, it (the government) would have come under criticism because the authorities had delayed decoding the message sent by the British chargé d'affaires in Beijing based on a definite information given to him about the possible sabotage of the Kashmir Princess. As a final attempt to influence RNK, all three—Willcox, Maxwell and the Governor of Hong Kong—impressed upon him the need to convey to the Chinese, particularly Zhou Enlai, about how assiduously the Hong Kong Police had pursued the case. Clearly, they wanted to use RNK, and through him, India, as an ally against the Chinese suspicions.

Amidst all these pressures, RNK left for his second and final visit to Beijing on 25 August 1955. On 27 August,

Zhou Enlai summoned him for the much-awaited meeting. RNK was accompanied by Bahadur Singh, Counsellor in the Indian Embassy, in Beijing since Ambassador Raghavan was busy with a pre-scheduled meeting. The most distinct memory that RNK had about the meeting was that it lasted for nearly three hours. The Chinese Premier was assisted by the then Vice Foreign Minister, Chang Han Phu, Hsiung and Zhou Enlai's interpreter. A lot of time was wasted in translation of the conversation. But more than anything else, RNK remembered, how the Chinese Premier was suspicious of the British attitude towards the investigation and how he thought the probe was flawed.

First up, the Chinese Premier asked RNK what he thought about the investigations so far. RNK, under instructions to be absolutely factual, replied that he would confine himself to the developments in the days after Hsiung had left Hong Kong—which was on 10 August—and talk about the information that the Hong Kong Police had shared with him informally. RNK also told him that according to his understanding, the Hong Kong authorities would soon submit a formal report to the Chinese Government. Zhou was not convinced. RNK noted, 'On this (hearing Kao's remark), Zhou Enlai made the surprising remarks that it was hard to say whether the Chinese Government will receive the report, as he considered it possible that the Hong Kong Government might not inform even the results of the enquiries. I countered this by saying that my personal impression was that the Hong Kong Police could not afford to maintain complete silence about it.'

The Chinese Premier was not convinced. He asked RNK what he thought would be the next course of action by the Hong Kong authorities—whether they would lapse into inactivity and, subsequently, close the case by the end of 1955. Kao refused to take the bait. He refrained from making any comment on the political aspect. Instead, he told Zhou Enlai that in his estimation, the Hong Kong Police had done a fair job under the circumstances so far. 'I confessed to Zhou Enlai that there had been a period when I felt disheartened by the apparent lack of communication on the part of the Hong Kong Police regarding the day-to-day happening, but my overall impression was that they had not relaxed in their effort to unravel the case,' Kao noted.

Zhou, however, continued to press his point and said he had information about two officers of the Hong Kong Special Branch who, according to him, were secretly in league with the KMT. He felt that had it not because of these two officers, the case would have been solved much quicker. 'The Hong Kong Government seemed to believe more in the agents of the KMT than in the information given by him personally,' the Chinese Premier remarked. 'There are clearly political reasons for this attitude of the British Government and these reasons are connected to developments in world politics,' an angry Zhou ranted. A careful Kao told him that he could only share what was in his direct knowledge and that these views were not to be taken either as those of the Hong Kong Government or the Government of India. Zhou, however, would not give up easily. He, in fact, asked RNK, 'Can we put it this way? The Hong Kong authorities knew that you were going to leave Hong Kong and would return to India via Beijing. Is it possible that they wanted to 'bluff' you regarding the present state of the investigation?' RNK replied, 'Anything is possible. But my personal assessment was that substantial progress had been made in the investigation of the case. This somewhat angered Mr Zhou Enlai who felt that I seemed to question his assessment. He averred with some heat that if in the event he was proved right, then it would mean that I had been deceived by the Hong Kong Government,' RNK noted. Holding his ground against an aggressive Zhou, RNK continued to listen to the Chinese Premier who remained sceptical of the British attitude towards the investigation.

Before concluding the meeting, Zhou tried another gambit. He asked RNK if he would write a joint report with Hsiung, since both had liaised closely in Hong Kong. The ever-cautious Kao simply said that he would let Delhi know of the matter and work according to directions given to him. Delhi promptly said no to the proposal and told Kao not to get 'entangled' in the matter. Hsiung also tried to persuade RNK to change his mind but to no avail. Finally, it was decided that Hsiung will write a report, which RNK would read through and suggest corrections informally without getting associated officially.

The next day, Kao was invited for a special dinner with the Premier at the summer palace outside Beijing. It was a special honour for a relatively junior officer, but the dinner invitation impressed India's ambassador and Bahadur Singh. Zhou Enlai was in his charming self. He thanked RNK for his effort and involvement. Kao's Kashmir Princess sojourn was about to end.

RNK returned to Hong Kong and briefed the Police Commissioner, the head of Special Branch and the Governor on his Beijing trip. Kao also had two lengthy meetings with Hanley. 'My discussions with Mr Hanley were particularly interesting because being in the same kind of trade, we could talk without reservations and with the full confidence that our respective views would be fully understood and appreciated,' Kao noted.

Interestingly, in his notes, RNK has a detailed take on the KMT operation in Hong Kong, although he does not mention who gave him the information or how he obtained the inputs. Clearly, his curiosity and training played major a part in Kao getting the full details of KMT's presence in Hong Kong.

It was discovered that the KMT intelligence organization, called the Fifth Liaison Group, had been functioning in Hong Kong from a certain address in Temple Street behind the cover of an electrical shop. The object of this group was to work as an agency for securing KMT agents who were to be infiltrated into China, and also to arrange facilities for their travel and for the transmission of their reports. The owner of this shop, called Kwan Tsau Kee, was in a small way connected with the activities of this group, but the two main workers of this group were Tang Po Ting and Tsang Yat Nin. Two people who were also known to this group and who visited the shop often were Kwan Mao Kung and Chao San Yu.

Meanwhile, by early 1955, the Bandung Conference was constantly in the news since it was going to be the first of its kind gathering of world leaders from Asia and Africa. The Chinese were reported to be sending a large contingent to the conference. This is where the entire episode appears to have become interesting.

Sometime in March 1955, a man called Wu was reported to have got in touch with the Fifth Liaison Group of the KMT intelligence network at Temple Street in Hong Kong. Around 10 March, Wu met one Kwan Tsau and Tsang Yat Nin from whom he inquired whether they had a relative or friend working at the Hong Kong airport, who could undertake a job of national importance for him.

Kwan informed Wu that he knew of no such person, but when this matter was later discussed with another colleague of theirs, Ghou Tsang Yu, he said that he had a man called Chou Chu working at the airport. This information was passed on by Kwan Mao Kung to Tsang Yat Nin, who took Kwan Mao Kung, on 18 March, to meet Wu at a coffee shop. The proprietor of the electrical shop was also present at this meeting. On 25 March, another meeting took place between Wu, Chou Tsang Yu and Tsang Yat Nin.

In the following three days, meetings were held between Chou Tsang You and Chou Chu, who was later introduced to Wu. Wu made some preliminary proposals of relatively harmless nature and having accrued Chou Chu's confidence, finally asked him whether he would undertake to sabotage a Communist plane. Substantial rewards and safety in Taiwan were promised. In the beginning, Chou Chu refused to undertake the task saying that it was too dangerous. Later, however, Wu seems to have persuaded Chou Chu to agree to do this assignment and promised to give him a reward of 600,000 Hong Kong dollars.

There were several meetings again in various hotels between Chou Chu and, at least, two others. At these meetings, Chou Chu was given various sums of money and also trained in the use of a time bomb. Finally, the bomb was handed over to him wrapped in brown paper, at the hotel, by a man named Wong. On 10 April, while servicing the Air India international plane, the Kashmir Princess, Chou Chu planted the bomb with the help of a colleague. The bomb exploded in mid-air, leading to the crash of the Kashmir Princess as detailed earlier. As far as Chou Chu was concerned, his job was well done. But Wu decided not to pay the promised amount to Chou Chu, who in frustration and fear, smuggled himself out on a cargo plane to Taiwan, almost a month after the sabotage.

Kao had also managed to get a fair idea about who Wu was through his contacts in the Special Branch of the Hong Kong Police. Apparently, Wu was actually Wu Yinchin, a resident of Shanghai, but someone who had made Hong Kong his home in the previous two years. Investigations had revealed that Wu had deep connections with the KMT's intelligence network, and that he also handled enormous amount of money to fuel the KMT intelligence operations in Hong Kong and also in parts of mainland China.

And yet, the Hong Kong Police could not arrest either the main conspirator or Chou Chu, the man who executed the conspiracy. However, for nearly six months after his return to

India in mid-September 1955, RNK kept getting occasional updates from Willcox about the progress or lack of it in the investigation. In January 1956, the British Government in London announced its inability to extradite Chou Chu to Hong Kong since the KMT authorities had refused to hand him over, although the 31 Taiwanese who were detained in Hong Kong for their connection with the Kashmir Princess case had been deported to Taiwan. A British Officer in Delhi told Kao that 13 others were still under arrest in Hong Kong.

It was now clear that the case was winding down with no apparent closure. In the middle of 1956, the Governor of Hong Kong, Sir Alexander Granthom, while passing through Delhi on his way to London, met RNK at the British High Commissioner's residence. From that conversation, and later from a chat with the representative of MI5 posted in Delhi, Kao realised that the Hong Kong authorities had prolonged the probe, made some efforts to get to the bottom of the conspiracy but eventually they had reached a dead end. To RNK, this now appeared to be the end of the matter.

Kao could not help but recall his last meeting with Zhou Enlai in which he had expressed his doubt over the sincerity of the Hong Kong authorities in pursuing the investigation and prosecuting the perpetrators. 'Now, in the event, it so happened that he was proved uncannily correct and the British were able to prosecute neither Chou Chu nor Wu and, in fact, the case was just wrapped up, as Zhou Enlai had said,' Kao noted.

In the end, RNK noted, apart from his written report to B.N. Mullik, he was also given personal audience by Prime

Minister Nehru. 'He was good enough to invite me to tea one afternoon at the Teen Murti House. For nearly two hours, I gave him a detailed account of what had transpired regarding this case since I had met him last in Bandung. At the end of my story, I remember, I said that I was much impressed with the courtesy and personal considerations, which Mr Zhou Enlai and other Chinese officials had shown to me. His reply was significant, and its full importance became clear to me only in the light of events which unfolded some years later culminating in the armed conflict between China and India in 1962. I distinctly remember that in reply to this observation of mine, Panditji had said, "Yes when they want to, the Chinese can be very polite and charming",' RNK wrote.

Nearly four decades later, *The China Quarterly*, a scholarly journal of the SOAS University of London, published a research paper on the Kashmir Princess episode, based mainly on British archives. It shed light on the motive of the assassination plot against Zhou Enlai and the global situation prevailing then. Steve Tsang, a researcher, wrote, 'The first half of 1955 was a testing time diplomatically for the KMT regime on Taiwan. Chiang Kai-shek admitted privately to his supporters in the Koumintang that the three-month period, from April to June, was the most precarious time for the ROC's (Republic of China or Taiwan's) diplomacy.'

The importance that Chiang Kai-shek attached to this period was because of the change of tactics by the People's Republic of China (China). After attacking some islands that belonged to China, in 1954, Beijing had decided to pursue peaceful means. Zhou Enlai was leading the initiative on China's behalf.

According to *The China Quarterly*, 'In Chiang Kai-shek's eyes Zhou had two objectives: First, he wanted to persuade the United States to negotiate with the PRC [People's Republic of China], isolate Chiang's regime and neutralise the effects of the mutual defence treaty which his government had recently signed with the United States, Secondly, he tried to nullify the efforts to prevent the PRC from joining the United Nations. Chiang was also concerned about the British Commonwealth policy towards the Taiwan question, and the improvement in relations between Britain and the PRC...

Tsang contends that from Chiang's point of view, in early 1955, Britain was attempting to clear the ground for the PRC to enter the United Nations. In his calculation, Zhou's peace offensive ... was at least as dangerous as, if not more grievous than, the military confrontation in the Taiwan Straits. Having just persuaded the United States to guarantee Taiwan's security by signing a mutual defence treaty, Chiang feared the British invitation for the PRC to join the United Nations would be the thin end of the wedge, which could only lead to either or a two China situation or United Nations trusteeship over Taiwan...'[1]

In the circumstances, as *The China Quarterly* commented, Chiang Kai-shek had every incentive to assassinate Zhou Enlai, who could have caused greater havoc for him than the People's Liberation Army. A successful assassination operation

---

[1] Steve Tsang, 'Target Zhou Enlai: The "Kashmir Princess" Incident of 1955', *The China Quarterly* 139 (September 1994), 766–782.

could greatly undermine the PRC's peace offensive... An attempt on Zhou's life staged in British Hong Kong, whether it was successful or not, could have added advantage of driving a wedge between the British and the PRC and put an end to their diplomatic flirtation started by Zhou and Sir Anthony Eden in Geneva. It would also provoke the PRC to accuse the United States of complicity, thus stiffening American resolve against admitting the PRC to the United Nations.

On the question of any prior knowledge that Zhou or the PRC had about the assassination plot, Tsang contends that Zhou and his government were aware of this murder plot before it happened, yet they chose not to take all the necessary measures to prevent it. 'In March 1955, shortly after Wo Yi-Chin (Wu, in Kao's notes) activated the Number 5 Liaison Group in Hong Kong, the People's Republic of China authorities already knew that Secret Service organizations of the US and Chiang Kai-shek were planning to carry out sabotage against their delegation to the Bandung conference...'[2]

In conclusion, Steve Tsang says, 'There is no doubt that KMT agents organised the assassination, and PRC agents knew of it beforehand. Both sides achieved part of their objectives, but the PRC came out on top. By successfully blowing up the Kashmir Princess, the Nationalist Secret Service boosted its own moral and provoked a renewed Communist propaganda against the Americans. Chiang Kai-shek, however, failed in his primary objectives. Zhou Enlai was missed as a target, the PRC's chance of joining the United

---

[2] Ibid.

Nations was not affected and Anglo-Chinese relations were not damaged. The PRC managed to rid Hong Kong of a significant number of nationalist agents, won the propaganda battle and gained better understanding of Hong Kong's policy and Britain's sincerity at a cost of 8 cadres. On moral grounds both sides were losers.'[3]

With such high stakes, India was the unlikely important part of the triangle and Kao was lucky to be working in the midst of such a high-level political and diplomatic tussle between different powers.

RNK spent around six months on the Kashmir Princess investigation. The time that he spent in the company of the Chinese and the British officers helped him establish a reputation for a quiet but effective working style and a life-long professional association with many in the British and the Chinese intelligence establishments.

[3] Ibid.

# SIX

# Of Observing People and Places

Hong Kong presented several difficulties to RNK and his companions. The team had landed there at the end of April, which, apparently, coincided with the period of acute water scarcity. Running water was available only for a couple of hours per day. 'I also realised that I did not have the right type of clothes , so as soon as I drew my first travelling allowance advance, we went to a tailor called Saklani on the Kowloon side, not far from Nathan Road, where I had a couple of suits made. I also had a couple of terylene shirts made of the wash-and-wear variety after which I was ready to live in Hong Kong for as long as necessary,' Kao noted in his recollection.

Hong Kong, then under British control, had a mixed population of Chinese-origin businessmen, Europeans and even Indian business community among others. On observing the ways different communities lived, Kao wrote,

'While the poor Chinese in Hong Kong, mainly refugees from Communist China, lived in conditions of unbelievable squalor and crowded in hovels and huts, which they had temporarily built covering the whole hillside, richer Chinese lived in luxurious comfort. They were the members of the prosperous overseas Chinese community. And their love of luxury and sensuous pleasure, seemed to me, was in sharp contrast to the austerity which Indian businessmen, mainly the Marwaris, practiced or, at least, professed practicing.'

'This, in many ways, provided a key to the difference in outlook between Indians and the Chinese. Though we belong to the same continent and have a lot in common, while in Indian life, the accent is on metaphysics or has been on metaphysics and austerity or, at least, display austerity in public, the Chinese are intensely practical people who are not ashamed of pandering to their senses. An example of this is the extent to which they have gone to give pleasure to different senses. It was explained to me by a Chinese in Hong Kong that while music delighted the sense of hearing, painting and gardening delighted the sense of vision, scents that of smell, delicious food that of the taste buds, it was the Chinese who discovered ways of flattering the sense of touch. And this led to the creation of small ball-like objects out of smooth jade, which the Manchu and Ming emperors kept in the palms of their hands and kept on rolling them constantly to give them sensuous satisfaction of the sense of touch. This also explains the almost complete lack of inhibition which the Chinese have about the food they partake, so long as it is good to taste or is reported to have good qualities.'

RNK had a different take on the Indians living in Hong Kong in the 1950s. They could be divided amongst two main groups—one was that of the Sindhi businessmen and the other was the remnants of the large number of Sikhs, rather Punjabis, who had joined the Hong Kong Police before the Japanese invasion. The latter mainly did relatively low paid jobs, mostly as watchmen in banks, shops and other business establishments.

To RNK, the Sindhi businessmen, most of whom belonged to the Bhaiban community, seemed to symbolise the nouveau riche, as they were loud and flashy, and the men adorned themselves with all kinds of gold bracelets and necklaces.

'What I found quite nauseating was the habit of Sindhi young men, mainly the shop assistants, of wearing kohl in their eyes, and who spoke with an affected English accent which was totally unpleasant.' However, by and large, Kao found them to be friendly people, who tried to be nice to visitors from India. 'I would be ungrateful if I did not acknowledge the hospitality that I received at the houses of many of them,' he wrote.

Kao had an interesting take on the contrast between Hong Kong and Communist China. 'It (Hong Kong) was a very wicked city, where everything could be bought and sold and everyone was, in a very cynical manner, engaged in the remorseless pursuit of wealth. In many ways, the mainland (Communist) China stood for something which was in stark contrast. The moment you entered China, gone was all the polish, glamour, colours, scintillatingly illuminated advertisements and the claptrap of consumer society. Instead of that, you could see hordes and hordes of young people with intent expression on their faces, all of them in blue boiler suits, men and women dressed alike in loose tunics and loose trousers,' he noted.

In Hong Kong, he had noticed that the Chinese women were chic. By comparison, he noted, the Europeans looked somewhat coarse. 'If you were in Hong Kong for three or four weeks, you would suddenly realise that European women looked somewhat coarse as compared to the smart chic and better dressed Chinese woman. Their general built was slim, skin was ivory-coloured, complexion clear and their straight, long limbs could not fail to impress even the casual visitor,' RNK remarked.

He contrasts this with an apt observation about Communist China and its women. 'Now, the same people lived in mainland China but their dress was totally different. The women there were completely innocent of any perfume or cosmetics; of course, they pretended to despise these as symptoms of a decadent capitalism. Yet, I cannot believe that even in the heart of the most ardent Chinese women cadres, there was no desire whatsoever to prettify themselves.'

RNK made only two visits to mainland China and spent the maximum time in Beijing, but his keen eye noticed the dilapidated condition of many of its buildings and roads that marked China's capital city and the difficulty of living. 'My first impression of Beijing was that it was a flat, calm and a very large sprawling city, with most buildings being of single storey, except for a few relatively new government structures.

The roads were wide. On my first visit itself, I noticed that many walls of buildings were in disrepair and footpath along the minor streets were broken. Somehow, the city did manage to convey an impression of scrupulous cleanliness in the sense that throughout the vast sprawling metropolis, you would not find a single piece of trash lying on the road and in some streets, even fallen leaves had been carefully swept aside,' he noted, concluding that the cleanliness was achieved through mass mobilisation.

Interestingly, like in current times, housing for all in Beijing was a challenge. And couples faced problems finding a house.

'The living conditions for the young people in China were very difficult, housing in particular. From the casual enquiries which I made from my interpreters, who are young people, I discovered that many of them could not marry because they did not have a place of their own to live in. Some of these people who were married were unable to keep their families with them. The men lived in men dormitories and their wives lived in women dormitories, even if they were posted in the same city. Quite often, of course, they were posted in towns several 100 miles apart,' RNK observed.

'On the roads, there were hardly any cars since only diplomats and high Chinese officials could own or use them. Most common Chinese people either walked or cycled their way around the vast city. There were a few old buses, mostly of East European origin, meant as public transport. The top officials used comfortable limousines adorned with curtains, so that the occupants of the car could not be seen by the commoners,' RNK noticed.

As a personal guest of Zhou Enlai, RNK, of course, had a car and two interpreters accompanying him. The hosts, as he has noted earlier, could turn on the charm offensive, when needed. To keep him occupied and entertained, the Chinese used to take Kao for elaborate meals and even arranged for visits to the Beijing opera and, of course, the mandatory sighting of the Great Wall of China.

At the opera, RNK had some interesting observations. 'It was explained to me that Beijing opera had stereotypical characteristics of an opera, and the villain could be identified from his attire and the way he wore his hair. Similarly, the hero also had a characteristic dress. Then, I was told that women parts were also played by men. It would be interesting here to recall that Zhou Enlai, as a young man, used to play parts of women in some classical Beijing opera pieces. But the Chinese music left me somewhat cold because that high nasal tone did not inspire me at all. And their instrumental music, quite often, except for the real classical tunes, seem to me rather cheap copy of western music,' he noted.

During Kao's first trip to Beijing, V.K. Krishna Menon, Nehru's confidante and India's representative at the UN, also happened to be on a visit to China. Zhou Enlai hosted a dinner in his honour. The hosts, who were aware that Menon was a vegetarian, had laid out an elaborate menu and seemed determined to go out of their way to impress Menon and others.

Kao's observation of the dinner is apt. 'Here, I saw an example of what might be called the high watermark of Chinese hospitality and the incident was an object lesson indicating the extent to which the Chinese could go to please people who they, at that moment, considered their friends. In view of the fact that Mr Krishna Menon himself was a vegetarian, all the dishes were vegetarian, and the number of courses was as numerous as they are at any traditional formal Chinese banquet. The only difference was that various vegetables were produced, some dressed as chicken, some as fish, some as pork. The staple food was, of course, potatoes, cabbage and cauliflower. I must say that compared to Indian vegetarian food, I found Chinese vegetarian food somewhat unappetising. But the taste of the food at the banquet was a matter of relatively small importance. The main thing was that the Chinese had demonstrated their desire to please Mr Krishna Menon and to indicate to all the guests the high regard in which they held him, and also to indicate that the Chinese were true friends of people from the third world. It is to be remembered that at that time, China was trying to gain recognition in the international world, and they were very keen to project the desirable picture of sweet amiability,' Kao noted.

As an officer nominated directly by Prime Minister Nehru for a delicate task, Kao was fortunate to have gotten the exposure to different cultures, circumstances and people very early in his career. His innate intelligence, combined with appropriate training, helped him make enduring contacts and some friends in the secretive world of espionage, intelligence and police investigations. Those six months in Hong and China were indeed life-changing for RNK.

# SEVEN

# The Ghana Assignment

By 1957, RNK was well-settled in his job as the Prime Minister's security officer and was travelling frequently with Nehru, both nationally and internationally. It was during one of Nehru's trips to London for the Commonwealth Prime Ministers' Conference in July 1957 that an interesting conversation took place that took Kao to the newly-independent country of Ghana in Africa for an assignment.

According to RNK's own notes, the then Ghanaian Prime Minister Dr Kwame Nkrumah PC requested the Indian Prime Minister for assistance in establishing an external intelligence service for Ghana. 'It appears that about the same time or a little earlier, Mr Daniel A. Chapman, who was then the Secretary to the Prime Minister of Ghana and also Secretary to the Ghanaian Cabinet, had discussed the matter informally with Mr B.N. Mullik, Director Intelligence Bureau (DIB), Govt of India, who had then gone to London to attend the

Commonwealth Security Conference to sought his advice on the matter,' RNK wrote.

These two discussions were followed by a letter from Dr Nkrumah in October 1957 in which he indicated that Ghana was keen on sending two senior police officers for training in India. As suggested by the Ghanaian Prime Minister, one of these two officers would eventually head the External Intelligence Service. In the same letter, he had requested services of an experienced Indian officer to be stationed in Ghana for a year or so to help Ghana establish the new organisation. 'The idea was that the expert should be the new head of the Service temporarily and lay down the foundation of the organisation. He should simultaneously train the senior police officers and select other staff required for establishing the service. Dr Nkrumah's suggestion was examined at length in the Ministry of External Affairs and home as also by Mr Mullik ... who was at service to service level also in contact with his colleagues in London particularly because this matter related to the establishment of a service in a Commonwealth country,' RNK noted.

After discussions across relevant ministries, Prime Minister Jawaharlal Nehru wrote back to his Ghanaian counterpart in November 1957 accepting its suggestion of India helping Ghana to establish a foreign intelligence service. Nehru's letter included a detailed proposal prepared by Mullik for the scheme to roll-out in several stages. In the first stage, it was proposed that the DIB of India should visit Ghana for about two or three weeks to examine the position on the ground to prepare a detailed plan. Simultaneously, arrangements were to be made for two to three Ghanaian officers to be trained in external intelligence in India. In the third and final stage, a senior Indian officer would go to Ghana to join the Ghanaian officers trained in India, once they return home and set up the organisation in that country.

'The suggestion was that this Indian intelligence officer would stay in Ghana for about a year, and with the help of the two Ghanaian officers who were trained in India, he would gradually set up the service, select the staff and arrange for their local training. He would also supervise the operations during the time of its implementation,' RNK wrote this in his notes many years later.

He also recalled that in the 'Indian scheme of things, it was especially emphasised that it would be better if the Indian officer who would go to Ghana would be loaned in an advisory capacity and would not formally be the head of the Ghanaian Intelligence Service. It was felt that until a Ghanaian officer would be selected for this post, probably either as the Cabinet Secretary or the Ghanaian officer-in-charge, who would take up the responsibility of controlling the organisation, the Indian officer would only act as an adviser.'

To pursue this scheme, Kao was selected by B.N. Mullik to go to Ghana and was relieved from his routine work and put on special duty from February 1958. The British Government, who had security liaison with the Ghanaians, and the director of IB had meanwhile kept themselves informed about the developments. Kao said, 'even if in their [the British Government] heart of hearts they were perhaps unhappy that Ghana had asked India for foreign expert advice instead of asking the UK for one, yet they pretended to like this arrangement and tried, very suddenly, to guide the working of the scheme through personal hints and the lightest of suggestions.'

However, for various reasons, B.N. Mullik's departure to Ghana, which was the first stage of the scheme, got postponed and, finally, he never visited Ghana. Meanwhile, in accordance with the scheme, which had been sent to the government of Ghana on April 1958, two Ghanaian officers arrived in India. They were Paul Yankey, who held the rank of the Superintendent of Police and Ben Forje, who was the Deputy Superintendent of Police. Kao was nominated to train these two officers. H.J. Kriplani, another IB officer, who was then working as the Deputy Central Intelligence Officer, was RNK's assistant.

Describing the two Ghanaian officers, Kao wrote: 'Both of them belonged to the Nzema tribe to which Dr Nkrumah belonged. Their ancestral home was in southwestern Ghana. Both of them had joined the Ghana Police as foot constables and gradually worked their way up. Their formal education was somewhat limited but they could express themselves in English with a fair degree of fluency, although their vocabulary was limited. In the beginning, we had some difficulty in getting adjusted to the Ghanaian accent and also the special terms and phrases which were common in West Africa. It was also interesting for us to observe that the speeches of these officers were often punctuated with squeals and exclamations, which were quite eloquent in themselves. It was obvious right from the beginning that both these officers had won the confidence of Dr Nkrumah and were intensely loyal to him. They were also discreet and conscious of the fact that they had been selected by their leader to break ground in the field of foreign intelligence. Therefore, they were determined to do their best in India.'

Realising the importance of the project, Kao and his assistants tried to fall in line with this approach and tried to adjust the programme to suit the convenience of the visiting officers. He noted, 'We had, right from the beginning, recognised that it was more important for us to make a good impact on the Ghanaian officers and to make them feel that they were amongst friends. The actual theoretical knowledge which they acquired about foreign intelligence operations was regarded as a matter of secondary importance by us. In organising the scheme and implementing it, and also generally holding their hands and making them feel that they were amongst friends, I was fortunate enough to have an excellent team which was headed by a very distinguished officer of the IB named Krishnan Nair. He was very ably assisted by H.J. Kriplani.'

RNK, who was known for his sharp observation powers and the ability to size up people, had shown those traits early in his career. While commenting on the two officers from Ghana, he noted, 'But for the common tribal background and the fact that both of them belonged to the Ghana Police, Paul Yankey and Ben Forje were, in many ways, contrasting in nature. Yankey was a burly, smiling man, who was ready for a joke all the time but it was clear that his buff exterior concealed an alert and clever mind. He was observant and had a good memory. Ben Forje seemed less mercurial and was more of a stable, plodding type of officer, who had meticulous attention to detail and worked with extreme consciousness. I got to know both these officers not only in India but also during my stay in Ghana. They were my constant guides and companions and during the time that I spent with them, I developed not only high regard for both of these officers but also a degree of affection…'

Even as the two officers from Ghana were undergoing training, RNK's name was formally proposed to the Ministry of External Affairs (MEA) and the Ministry of Home Affairs (MHA) as the officer who should implement the scheme to set up the foreign intelligence service for Ghana. It got immediately approved in principle but as is common in government proceedings, a long argument, which lasted 'over weeks and months', followed in which the MEA tried to scale down the allowances and other facilities which Mullik had suggested should be given to RNK.

RNK noted in detail the objections that were raised. 'Keeping in mind my rank as the Deputy Director in the IB at that time, he [Mullik] had suggested that I should draw my basic salary at the same rate as I was drawing in India but then it should be fixed according to the foreign scale and that I should be given a foreign service allowance and other facilities as was given to regular diplomats posted for the Indian mission in Ghana. This was stubbornly resisted by B.K. Kapur who the High Commissioner of India to Ghana at that time and, later, I discovered that his greatest anxiety was to ensure that my overall emoluments and facilities should in no way work out to be higher than what he himself was getting as the High Commissioner of India to Ghana.

'His approach in this matter was based on the assumption that for all practical purposes I was working in Ghana as a member of his mission and, therefore, it was only logical that my status, and consequently my pay and allowances, should be lower than those admissible to the High Commissioner. Here, he seemed to have missed the point because it was never the intention either of the Government of India or the Government of Ghana that I should work, in any way, as a part of the Indian High Commission in Ghana. My services were to be placed completely at the disposal of the Ghanaian government.'

Even as this bureaucratic tussle was on, there was a small development which was noticed by the IB. *The Tribune*, now headquartered in Chandigarh but was based out of Ambala, carried a news item originating from Accra (it is not clear from Kao's notes if it was *The Tribune's* own report or was sourced from an international news agency) that reported the Government of Ghana had decided to set up a committee to review national security with the help of Britain, Canada and Pakistan. RNK noted, 'This intrigued us immensely because we felt that if we were advising Dr Nkrumah regarding foreign intelligence, then there could hardly be any scope for Pakistan to be a member of the committee set up to deal with security matters pertaining to Ghana. Discreet enquiries were made about the matter and, later, it was concluded that there was no truth to the report. As far as I know, no action was taken for that and it was not followed up.' But the IB was wrong in its conclusion as RNK himself later wrote. 'In May 1958, the office of the Prime Minister of Ghana did issue a press release in which they confirmed that it has been decided to establish a committee of this type to deal with the national security and that they received cooperation from the government of UK, Canada and Pakistan in this regard. The note said that the committee will be composed of Sir Robert Hutchins, Chairman, Brig Fazil Mukin Khan of the Pakistan army and Mr L Bingham, a senior officer of the Royal Canadian mounted police. Some Ghanaians were to be associated with this too. Though I spent over a year in Ghana, I never got to know what precisely this committee did. So for all practical purposes in connection with the scheme with which I was involved, this matter could be completely ignored.'

Meanwhile, the bureaucracy continued to bicker over the perks and allowances for Kao's assignment in Ghana. Kao recalled that there were several occasions when he 'was on the point of losing interest in the proposal altogether'. Kao, in fact, requested the DIB to drop his name at least on two occasions. However, Mullik continued to press for an early resolution. Finally, a compromise was worked out. It was not something that the IB and RNK were happy about. Kao said that Mullik, however, advised him to accept whatever was offered to avoid 'all-round embarrassment'. RNK accepted Mullik's advice—when he could have declined to go—which portayed Kao's ability to put national interest above self-interest early in his career. As he himself noted, 'Though my enthusiasm had considerably subsided and my interest dulled, I felt that as it was in the nation's interest that India should help Ghana to establish a foreign intelligence service, I told Mr Mullik that I would go.'

There was another complication to be taken care of before Kao departed for Accra. The Ghana government wanted RNK to be on deputation for two years, but Mullik said he could not let Kao go for more than a year. Additionally, Kao did not want to give up the house he was then staying but the according to the rules of the government rule, no house could be kept for anyone for more than six months, if not posted in Delhi! So the IB and Kao worked out a neat arrangement. 'Since I did not wish to lose the government accommodation which I had in Delhi at 93, Lodhi Estate, where I was staying at that time, it was agreed that I would serve my period in Ghana in instalments of six months and at the end of first six months, I would return to India on leave at the Ghana government's expense. During this period, the Ghana government would go through the motion of trying to obtain my services again and I would go back on fresh deputation,' Kao wrote candidly.

Hence, after completing the formalities back home, the Kao couple embarked on their foray to Africa on an Air India flight to Rome from where they were to take a connecting BOAC (British Overseas Airways Corporation) flight to Accra. As luck would have it, they had to stay in Rome for more than ten days because the crew of the British airliner went on a strike. Recalling their adventure in Rome, Kao wrote, 'In the beginning, my wife and I were rather dismayed at the sudden breakdown of our travel arrangements, more so because we feared that we would run short of money but the Indian embassy in Rome were kind enough to come to our rescue and made arrangements for our daily allowances, while the BOAC, who are responsible for our detention in Rome, paid the hotel bill. Ultimately, this turned out to be an enforced holiday in Rome, which, I must confess, was not entirely unenjoyable.'

After the little break in Rome, RNK and Malini Kao arrived in Accra on 25 October 1958. They were received by one Mr Grant, who was the acting Foreign Secretary in the absence of the Foreign Secretary Yaw Idu, who was on leave at that time. The others who came to the airport to receive the couple included a protocol officer from the Foreign Ministry, along with Yankey and Forjoe, the two Ghanaians who had undergone a four-month training in India earlier that year, and the second secretary of the Indian High Commission in Accra.

As the Kao couple settled down in a nice house allotted to them, with two servants at their disposal, RNK discovered in a couple of days after arriving in Ghana that Yankey and Forjoe had done absolutely nothing since their return from India. They did not even report to the government of the training they had received from India. Everything had been kept pending for someone to come from India. 'I found myself in a situation where I had to make a big inning from scratch, as there was nothing on the ground, whatsoever, when I reached Accra—not even an office table, stationary items or a typist. Everybody was, however, cheerful and being unfailingly courteous. Every day, I was assured that everything would be taken care of,' Kao noted. However, the two Ghanaians who were trained in India had got the possession of a house—apparently suggested to them by the Prime Minister himself—to set up the headquarter. 'When I arrived there, there was nothing except three tables, three chairs and a telephone in the house,' Kao recalled.

Within the next few days, Kao learnt that the Ghanaian Prime Minister had himself selected 21 people, age ranging from 21 to 49 years, who were to be taken into the new organisation. Curiously, not one of them was a graduate and all of them were at that time employed in one capacity or another. The most intriguing thing was that the list had no police officer. One of them was working in the Trade Union Congress and another was an employee of the Convention People's Party, the then ruling party in Accra. Meanwhile, Kao discovered that the British intelligence officer and another British named Mckay, who was in charge of the Ghanaian Special Branch, were making special efforts to be friendly to him. This somewhat reminded Kao of the situation he had encountered in Hong Kong three years earlier when he had gone there to investigate the Kashmir Princess Case. The attention which he was receiving from the British was not only very welcoming and reassuring but also substantially useful. 'I much appreciated the courtesy and friendliness which I received from all the persons concerned, especially McKay and a gentleman called John Thomson,' Kao wrote. Interestingly, while Kao found McKay and Thomson useful, frank and sincere, they had different personalities and adopted different approaches in dealing with Kao.

A sharp observer of human nature and their characteristics, Kao noted, 'At the outset, however, I should mention that my first reaction in meeting British officers and businessmen in Ghana was somewhat of disappointment because on the whole it appeared to me that the British who went to West Africa were not of the same class as the British Civil servants and the British traders who went to India. This is understandable because it must not be forgotten that while India was regarded as the jewel in the British Crown, West Africa, for a number of years because of its bad climate, was known as the white man's grave.' RNK also had a thing or two to say about McKay and Thomson.

McKay had served in the Second World War and had been in Palestine when it was divided. He was a man of medium build with a freckled face and ginger hair. To Kao, he looked like an Irishman. Kao observed, ' Though he (McKay) had a quick temper, I think he had a heart of gold. It was somewhat pathetic to see these people were serving their terms in Ghana because it was clear to me that when the wind of change which was blowing throughout Africa these colonial servants felt out of place and unwanted. Considering that McKay had got four small children and a wife to support and that he had no special qualification besides his experience in the police, I think he faced up to this situation fairly well and during my stay in Ghana he continued to serve the Ghana government faithfully. Later, after my return from Ghana, I remained irregularly in touch with him and the last time I heard from him, he was in Swaziland in South Africa.'

John Thompson was slightly a different kind of person. According to Kao's observation, he was a true-bred Englishman, who was quite bossy-looking, tall and a bachelor. He had a university degree since he belonged to the old Sudan Civil Service, which, in some ways, 'approximated though it was a poor second to the Indian civil service.' RNK felt, 'In any case John Thompson had more characteristics of an empire builder and at this point was somewhat emphasised by the fact that he had with him a bearer call Abdullah whom he had brought from Khartoum.'

As he encountered these diverse characters during his first few days in Accra, RNK was still waiting to see the prime minister. Finally, almost a week after he had arrived in Accra, Dr Nkrumah met Kao in his office. One of the first things RNK told him was the inability of DIB Mullik in visiting Ghana. However, Kao assured the Ghanaian prime minister of his and India's full commitment to help Ghana establish the Foreign Intelligence Service.

Dr Nkrumah was a man of medium height and medium built. He had a prominent forehead and bright large eyes. Kao's own assessment of the Ghanian prime minister was that he was supremely self-assured and it was obvious that he considered himself a man of destiny who was to lead Africa in the struggle to realise their own distinctive personality. Doctor Nkrumah spoke and wrote English with great facility and was a good public speaker, particularly in his own language, and he was very eloquent and could sway the mass. RNK found Dr Nkrumah in a very neat well-cut two-piece suit. He wore fresh, white shirt and a bright, knotty tie, and it was clear that he paid considerable attention to his wardrobe. Kao's first meeting with the Ghanian prime minister was in the castle where he lived and held his office. The castle had been the official residence as well as the office of the British governor during the colonial days.

As they settled down to discuss the task ahead, RNK asked the Prime Minister Nkrumah about his priorities. From his reply, it was clear that Dr Nkrumah wanted the Foreign Intelligence Service, later christened as Foreign Service Research Bureau or FSRB, to give first priority to the French-occupied territory that surrounded Ghana on its three sides. The next important thing, according to him, was to be the United Arab Republic UAR. In this context, the Prime Minister added that the UAR embassy in Accra had been doing a lot of offensive intelligence work. The next in priority, he felt, should come the intelligence activities of the British and the Americans. On communism, Dr Nkrumah said that he did not want to give it too much attention at that moment because he felt it did not constitute an immediate problem. Of course, he accepted that the Soviets had put enormous pressure on him to establish an embassy in Accra. He informed that until then, he had managed to resist this pressure but added that he would be interested in receiving any assessment or review from RNK on matters of the Russian design and international communist activities. This is a subject on which he said the British had offered to help him too.

Slightly taken aback by the huge expectations that the Ghanaian leader had from him and India, RNK explained to him various aspects of intelligence. 'I recounted briefly to him the methods of work and the difference in the scope of positive intelligence and counterintelligence. He promptly said that he would like me to advise him on both, and that I should also see what the Special Branch under my care had been doing,' Kao noted in his recollection.

RNK continued, 'In my talk with the Prime Minister, I impressed upon him the importance of training and hinted that we might have to get some staff for this from India as well as some office people to organise the main registry. He immediately asked me to prepare a scheme and promised all assistance.'

Kao confessed being somewhat overwhelmed by the magnitude of the task suggested to him by the Prime Minister Nkrumah, and the total burden of responsibility which had he placed on RNK's shoulders by promising to accept his advice totally. Kao remarked, 'In a manner, he seemed so sincere that it never had crossed my mind that this could be opposed. In fact, it was not. I must record here that during my more than one year of stay in Ghana, I never had even the slightest suspicion of dubiousness or duplicity in Dr Nkrumah's behaviour towards me. He was frank, free and friendly.'

RNK got down to the basic tasks of raising a new organisation. The newly recruited Ghanaian officers had to be trained further. He had to encourage Yankey and Forjoe to run operations on their own. Other officers of the Bureau had to learn how to assess reports from the field, how to filter the truth from the embellishments of agents and how to prepare the finished product of the FSRB labours for the consumers, chiefly by the foreign ministry, but not always the Prime Minister.

Even as he was busy with training and raising the FSRB, Kao had to navigate his way through local politics, jealousies and palace intrigues. However, Dr Nkrumah's British Secretary, Erika Powell, made RNK's task easier by smoothening many wrinkles of daily functioning. Erika Powell, according to Kao, was 'devoted in mind, spirit and motion to Dr Nkrumah.' Kao wrote candidly about Erika—'She loved him, and she served him faithfully in every way possible.' However, Erika had to go back to England, 'a heartbroken and a defeated woman', after the Ghanian leader married an Egyptian Coptic lady.

During his stint in Ghana, however, Erika was a great tower of strength for RNK. He records it thus—'I received great kindness and consideration from her and I'm grateful for the tactful manner in which she unobtrusively removed various wrinkles, which a lot of people, for understandable reasons, tried to create in Accra while I was there. These persons were Ghanaians as well as a number of British officers. They regarded me as an intruder and somewhat resented the total trust which Dr Nkrumah had placed in me.'

As days and months passed, Kao gradually put in place a basic structure to run the newly-created FSRB. One year passed quickly. As planned, after six months, RNK and Malini Kao came back to India for a brief period and went back to Accra. By all accounts, they were a popular couple in the Ghanaian capital during their stint. But DIB Mullik wanted Kao back to do more pressing jobs in India. A replacement had to be found since India had committed to depute an officer for two years in Ghana.

By a strange quirk of fate, RNK's successor in Ghana turned out to be Kao's brother-in-arms, Sankaran Nair, who wasn't the first choice, incidentally.

As Nair narrates in his book, Mullik had chosen Amrit Midha to succeed Kao in Ghana. Midha had finished his training for the assignment. Nair was summoned by Joint Director Hooja, who was in charge of the training. He surprised Nair by revealing DIB's Mullik's new instruction that he (Nair) should go to Ghana and not Midha. A surprised Nair asked for time to accept the sudden assignment. After checking with his wife Indira, who had no objection, Nair thought of taking one more input. 'So I went to consult my friend philosopher and guide, Ramji, about the offer. He told me to accept the offer without any hesitation. I realised that his advice was one of the best that I had received. Exposure to foreign countries, foreign races, foreign customs, food and manners, I have found, is the best postgraduate education one can get. Such exposure demolishes racial prejudices, national arrogance and broadens the mental horizon,' Nair wrote.[1] The Nair couple landed in Accra in December 1959 and stayed till early 1961. Nair had an equally distinguished stint in Ghana like his mentor RNK. Apart from running and improving the efficiency of the FSRB, Nair as the Indian representative, was the centre of attention for many intelligence operatives stationed in Ghana. While the British representative had a

---

[1] K. Sankaran Nair, *Inside IB and RAW: The Rolling Stone that Gathered Moss* (New Delhi: Manas Publications, 2019).

close liaison with Nair, the Israelis who had wormed their way into Nkrumah's inner circle, approached Nair many times to convey a message about Israel's desire to open diplomatic relations with India. 'I said step the Israeli officials overture diplomatically as this was none of my business, so he lost further interest in me,' Nair remembered.[2]

Five years later, in 1966, both RNK and Nair had an interesting and what turned out to be their last encounter with Dr Nkrumah. As Nair wrote, 'In February 1966, years after I had left Ghana and returned to Delhi, Nkrumah went on an official visit to what was then Peking under Mao Tse Tung, halting en route to Delhi for a brief meeting with Mrs (Indira) Gandhi, who had become Prime Minister of India. The President of Ghana unwittingly embarrassed Mrs Gandhi by kissing her on the cheeks western style which Indians have not adopted. Kao and I were not official invitees for this. So while protocol greetings took place, the two of us stood aside till the Ghanaian President made his way to the ceremonial pandal. We then stepped out of the shadows and greeted Nkrumah who after a moment's hesitation recognised us and reciprocated our salutations with utmost affection. The protocol boys of the foreign ministry were wondering what sort of worms had creeped out of the woodwork. From Delhi, Nkrumah continued his journey to Peking the next day and shortly thereafter we heard that he had been overthrown by a military coup. Nkrumah never returned to his motherland and was given asylum by his friend, President Sekou Toure of neighbouring Guinea, which, for some years, had a tenuous

---

[2] Ibid.

union with Ghana. The Redeemer died some years later of cancer, a forgotten hero.'[3]

Thus ended India's Ghanaian dalliance but RNK and Nair's association—already strong—turned into a deep friendship because of their common 'Ghanaian heritage', which was to benefit India in later years when they founded the R&AW.

---

[3] Ibid.

# EIGHT

# The 1962 Shock and the Formation of ARC

The Indian debacle in the 1962 war with China prompted many changes in the Indian security establishment, especially in the intelligence set-up. The IB, which was the sole agency handling both internal and external intelligence, felt the need for specialised organisations that could look after the gathering of technical intelligence, run clandestine operations into Tibet and even operate behind enemy lines across the Himalayan frontier. As a result, two new important organisations—the Aviation Research Centre (ARC) and the Special Frontier Force (SFF)—were created under the IB.

The ARC was established on 4 June 1963, and RNK headed the organisation from 1 September 1963 until 1 November 1966.

The ARC was the product of an intelligence cooperation agreement between India and the US in the immediate aftermath of the 1962 war. Eight C-46 aircraft and four smaller planes with their pilots were deployed to a secret Indian air base, code named 'Oak Tree'. Now we know that it is at Charbatia in Odisha. Later, the ARC started operating from Sarsawa in Uttar Pradesh, Doomdooma in Assam and Palam in Delhi. Its task was to get photographic and technical intelligence from inside Tibet and Xinjiang.

The SFF was formed on 14 November 1962, a week before the Chinese declared a unilateral ceasefire. Initially, it was known as 'Establishment 22' or 'two-two' because its first chief, Major General Sujan Singh Uban, had earlier commanded the 22 Mountain Brigade, revealed author and historian Claude Arpi.[1]

On 19 November 1962, the Chinese Peoples' Liberation Army (PLA) had come close to Tezpur in the plains of Assam, having made almost unimpeded progress through the Kameng sector in the then North-East Frontier Agency (NEFA)—now the state of Arunachal Pradesh. Faced with this dire situation, Prime Minister Jawaharlal Nehru was seeking urgent military help from the US.

Arpi added, 'On 19 November, the day after Nehru sent two panicky letters to the US President, a crucial meeting to answer Nehru was held in the White House. The then Secretary of Defence Robert McNamara, the Secretary of State Dean Rusk, as well as his Assistant for Far Eastern Affairs, Averell Harriman, a most respected diplomat and politician, were present. The CIA bosses were also in attendance. The

---

[1] http://claudearpi.blogspot.com/2012/11/consigned-to-dustbin-of-history.html

declassified US archives tell us: "McNamara urged that the first move be to find out what the real situation was. If we were to put our prestige and resources at risk, we must find out the score. He proposed sending a small high-level military mission immediately to Delhi. including State and Intelligence people in order to concert a plan of action with the Indians.""[2]

Nehru's letter to then President of US, John F. Kennedy (JFK), was a desperate appeal to prevent the Chinese from taking control of the Northeast. He wrote, 'The situation in the NEFA command has deteriorated still further. Bomdila has fallen and the retreating forces from Sela have been trapped between Sela Ridge and Bomdila. With the advance of the Chinese in massive strength, the entire Brahmaputra Valley is seriously threatened and unless something is done immediately to stem the tide, the whole of Assam, Tripura, Manipur and Nagaland would also pass into Chinese hands. The Chinese have amassed massive forces in the Chumbi Valley between Sikkim and Bhutan another invasion from that direction appears imminent...'[3]

Nehru then went on to ask for immediate assistance in strengthening the Indian Air Force (IAF), which, he said, was not well equipped.

'We have repeatedly felt the need of using the air arm in support of land forces, but have been unable to do so as in the present state of our air and radar equipment, we have no

---

[2] Ibid.

[3] John F. Kennedy Presidential Museum and Library, Boston, National Security Files.

defence against retaliatory action by the Chinese. I therefore request that support be given immediately to strengthen our air arm sufficiently to stem the tide of the Chinese invasion.

"'I'm advised that for providing adequate air defence a minimum of 12 squadrons of supersonic all weather fighters are essential. We have no modern radar cover in this country. For this also we seek your assistance. Our needs are most immediate. The United States Air Force personnel will have to man these fighters and radar installations while our personnel are being trained..." Any action to be taken against the Chinese beyond the limits of our country for example in Tibet will be taken by IAF planes manned by Indian personnel...'[4]

McNamara's delegation arrived in India three days later; during their stay, the CIA officials held lengthy discussions with Mullik. According to Jonathan Knaus, author of *Orphans of the Cold War: America and the Tibetan Struggle for Survival*, the CIA station chief in India, 'The Indians were interested in the Tibet program because of its intelligence collection value... Mullik was particularly interested in paramilitary operations.' In the end, the Chinese declared a unilateral ceasefire on 20 November, obviating the necessity of immediate American military aid. Over the next six months, the Americans helped India in different ways.

The National Security Action Memorandum number 209, approved on 10 December 1962 by JFK, authorised a new military aid package for India. Under the aid programme, it was decided that the US would:

---

[4] Ibid.

1. Assist in creating and equipping six new mountain divisions to work with the Indian Army to guard the Himalayas.

2. To help India increase its own arms production facilities.

3. Prepare for a US-UK air defence programme for India. The first two missions were to assist India develop its capabilities and the third was a joint American-British military exercise in India. Kennedy wanted the funding for the program to be split evenly with the United Kingdom and its Commonwealth partners.[5]

Eventually, the Americans did provide military assistance to India, but the India-US cooperation was far better in clandestine operations with the help of SFF and ARC. According to Bruce Riedel, 'The CIA agreed to support the SFF with a clandestine air force. The SFF conducted cross border reconnaissance operations to place sensors for detecting nuclear and missile tests and devices for intercepting Chinese military communications.'[6] Arpi noted, 'Mullik and Des FitzGerald, the CIA's Far East division chief, agreed that the IB with CIA support would train a 5,000-strong tactical guerrilla force; the CIA's Far East Division would create a strategic long-range resistance movement inside Tibet and the Tibetan freedom fighters in Mustang (Nepal) would remain under the CIA's control.'[7]

---

[5] Bruce Riedel, *JFK's Forgotten Crisis: Tibet, The CIA and the Sino-Indian War* (Washington, D.C.: The Brookings Institution, 2015).

[6] Ibid.

[7] http://claudearpi.blogspot.com/2012/11/consigned-to-dustbin-of-history.html

Riedel claims Nehru was an enthusiastic supporter of the projects. 'He visited the main SFF training camp in the Himalayas on 14 November 1963 and the secret air base Oak Tree on 2 January 1964 to see the covert action first hand.

The second project for which India provided support was the training of Tibetans at Camp Hale in Colorado and at other CIA facilities before they were sent to Tibet. Over 135 Tibetans were trained there to operate behind Chinese lines in their homeland. The Indians were not eager for them to be parachuted into Tibet, however, because this action would be very provocative. Instead, the resistance fighters would infiltrate across the line of actual control with help from the Intelligence Bureau. Between 1964 and 1967, 25 teams of fighters were sent into Tibet. The members of one team survived for 2 years inside Tibet but the rest of the teams were either captured, killed or came back to India almost immediately after crossing the line of actual control. The project was abandoned in 1968.'[8]

Riedel said the CIA played the lead role in a third project, which was to revitalise the Tibetan force in Mustang. To coordinate all the three projects, a special centre within the IB was set up in New Delhi in November 1963. Despite much prodding by CIA, however, the Mustang force carried out almost no missions across the border into Tibet. It was gradually shut down by the CIA and the fighters helped to find new jobs in drug factories and hotels in Pokhra in Nepal. JFK was also fully briefed on them. 'In 1964 the

---

[8] John Kenneth Knaus, *Orphans of the Cold War: America and the Tibetan Struggle for Survival* (New York: PublicAffairs, 2000).

CIA was authorised 1,735,000 dollars for the joint projects, a significant amount for covert programs. But except for the SFF patrols, the project had little success,' Riedel quoted Knaus.

However, the joint IB-CIA programme had one positive fallout. Even as the ARC and SFF were getting off the ground, the Americans asked for permission to fly U-2 missions over Tibet and Xinjiang and Prime Minister Nehru approved this. While the ARC's primary assets, the C-46 aircraft, gathered intelligence on the PLA that proved useful to the Indian Armed Forces and its intelligence agencies, those over Xinjiang gave the Americans best available information on China's proposed nuclear test site at Lop Nur. In early 1964, a U-2 detachment was based at Charbatia at the ARC base. The U-2 plane flew several missions over western China to obtain imagery reports, confirming China's plan to test a nuclear device. Riedel said, 'On 26 August 1964, a special National Intelligence Estimate told President Lyndon Johnson (who had succeeded JFK), that on the basis of new overhead photography, we are now convinced that the previously suspect facility at Lop Nur in Western China is a nuclear test site which could be ready for use in about two months.'[9] Sure enough, China tested its first nuclear device at Lop Nor on 16 October 1964.

During this period, RNK, who was setting up ARC from scratch, established close contacts with American intelligence bureaucracy. For nearly two years, the ARC and American intelligence operatives and technical hands worked in tandem

[9] Bruce Riedel, *JFK's Forgotten Crisis: Tibet, The CIA and the Sino-Indian War* (Washington, D.C.: The Brookings Institution, 2015).

to make ARC one of the most effective and crucial TECHINT resources in Asia. After important overseas assignments in Ghana and Hong Kong and taking care of Prime Minister Nehru's security between 1959 and 1962, RNK would become an institution builder as the next decade would show.

(14621) Wt.11709/P.79 20,000 4/40 A.& E.W.Ltd. Gp.685

Any further communication on this subject should be addressed to—
The Under Secretary of State for India,
Services Department,
India Office,
& General. London, S.W. 1,
and the following reference quoted :—

S. & G. 5667/40.

*Telephone* :—
Whitehall 8140. I.O. Ext. No._____
*Telegrams* :—
Retaxandum, London.

**INDIA OFFICE,**

**WHITEHALL,**

**LONDON, S.W. 1.**

21 September, 1940.

Sir,

I am directed by the Secretary of State for India to inform you that he has appointed you to be a Probationary Assistant Superintendent of Police in the Indian Police with effect from 27th March, 1940.

2. During your probation you will be subject to the rules of which a copy is herewith enclosed.

3. The Secretary of State may at any time remove you from the Service if you fail to comply with these rules, or with any orders given to you by a duly constituted authority, or if on account of adverse reports upon your conduct or work, or for any other reason the Secretary of State may decide that you are not in all respects qualified for further employment in the Indian Police.

4. On the satisfactory completion of your period of probation you will be confirmed as an Assistant Superintendent of Police.

5. You will commence to draw pay on the time scale prescribed for the Indian Police and to earn leave from the date on which you reported yourself for duty to Government and your service for pension will count from the same date.

I am, Sir,
Your obedient Servant,

*Sadar*

Rameshwar Nath Kao, Esq.,

*Letter appointing Kao to the Indian Police,*
*issued from London*

## STATUTORY RULES AND ORDERS
### 1939 No. 476

## INDIA

THE INDIAN POLICE (CONDITIONS OF SERVICE OF PROBATIONERS APPOINTED IN INDIA) RULES, 1939. DATED APRIL 6, 1939.

———

I, Lawrence John Lumley, Marquess of Zetland, one of His Majesty's Principal Secretaries or State, in virtue of the powers conferred by Sub-section (1) of section 247 of the Government of India Act, 1935(**a**), hereby make, with the concurrence of my Advisers, the following rules, namely:—

**1.** (1) These Rules may be cited as "The Indian Police (Conditions of Service of Probationers appointed in India) Rules, 1939".

(2) They shall come into force on the 10th January, 1939.

**2.** In these Rules, "a probationer" means a person appointed after a general or limited competitive examination or by selection in India to the service of the Crown in India as a probationary Assistant Superintendent of Police who has not yet been confirmed as such under the provisions of these Rules.

**3.** On appointment a probationer shall be paid the sum of Rs. 400 towards the cost of uniform and outfit and shall, if the Government under which he is serving consider that he should maintain a horse be entitled to receive a free grant not exceeding Rs. 600 towards the cost of horse and saddlery.

**4.** A probationer shall within two years from the date on which he reported for duty pass such departmental examinations, including tests in riding, as the Government may prescribe, and if he fails to pass he may be removed from the service:

Provided that the Government may exempt any probationer from passing all or any of the prescribed examinations or may extend beyond two years the period within which they shall be passed, and in either event may authorise the payment to the probationer, on the expiry of the period of two years aforesaid, of any increments in pay to which he would have been entitled if he had passed the examinations within two years.

---

(**a**) 26 Geo. 5 & 1 Edw. 8. c. 2.

**5.** The pay of a probationer and his service for the purpose of calculating increments of pay in the time scale applicable to officers of the Indian Police shall commence from the date on which he reports for duty to Government.

**6.** A probationer shall conform to all the rules and regulations of the service which are applicable to a probationary Assistant Superintendent of Police.

**7.** A probationer who has satisfied the Government as to his conduct during probation and as to his practical aptitude for police duties, and has passed or been exempted from passing, the prescribed examinations, shall be confirmed as an Assistant Superintendent of Police, and shall thereafter be governed by the Rules and Regulations applicable to the Indian Police in force at the date of his appointment as a probationer.

Given under my hand this 6th day of April, 1939.

*Zetland,*

One of His Majesty's Principal
Secretaries of State.

LONDON
PRINTED AND PUBLISHED BY HIS MAJESTY'S STATIONERY OFFICE
To be purchased directly from H.M. STATIONERY OFFICE at the following addresses:
York House, Kingsway, London, W.C.2; 120 George Street, Edinburgh 2;
26 York Street, Manchester 1; 1 St. Andrew's Crescent, Cardiff;
80 Chichester Street, Belfast;
or through any bookseller

1939
Price 1*d.* net

(2990—7) Wt. 6—1 500 4/39 P. St. G. 416

*The rules and orders for Indian Police probationers
issued with the appointment letter*

*Kao (back row, third from left) with other officers sometime in the early 1940s*

*Kao in a rare smiling photo*

*From the Indian Police*
*to*
*The Indian Police Service*

With the dawn of Independence
on the midnight of August 14th, 1947,
Indian officers of the Indian Police assumed leadership of
the Police in India from the departing British officers
with a commitment and total dedication to,

**Defend the Honour, Security and Integrity of India.**

**Serve with Loyalty the Government & the Constitution of India.**

**Adhere to the Rule of Law.**

**Preserve Public Safety and Order.**

These officers of the Indian Police became the nucleus and
the moving spirit of the newly formed Indian Police Service
for meeting the many challenges before the Nation.

We, the surviving members, salute the memory of the
Indian Police.

We felicitate and congratulate the succeeding
Indian Police Service
for carrying forward these ideals and nursing to fullness
the high traditions of the Service.

| | | | |
|---|---|---|---|
| V. G. KANETKAR | D. G. BHATTACHARYYA | P. K. SEN | K. F. RUSTAMJI |
| S. B. SHETTY | N. RAMA IYER | TRILOK NATH | A. G. RAJADHYAKSHA |
| F. V. ARUL | R. N. KAO | B. CHATTERJEE | E. S. MODAK |
| A. K. DAVE | ASHWINI KUMAR | R. K. GUPTA | K. SANKARAN NAIR |

*A pledge by the 16 Indian Police officers, including Kao and Sankaran
Nair, who formed the nucleus of the newly formed IPS*

*A serious, almost reluctant, Kao posing for a photo at home.
Notice an artistic painting behind him*

Kao at the ultra-secret Special Frontier Force (SFF) facility.
IG SS Uban also seen in both pictures

Handsome as
ever even in
old age

The stylish
gentleman

*Kao taking a rare guard of honour at an undisclosed location*

*Mrs Gandhi with Kao, G.C. Saxena (later, a R&AW chief)
and G.B.S. Sidhu*

*Kao at the ground breaking ceremony for the new R&AW building.*
*Sankaran Nair to his right in the second photo*

No.A.19012/3/81-Ad.I
Government of India
Cabinet Secretariat
Rashtrapati Bhavan

———

New Delhi, the 11th August, 1981

To

Shri R.N. Kao
E/10-2 Vasant Vihar
New Delhi.

Subject:- Offer of appointment as Senior
Adviser in the Cabinet Secretariat.

———

Sir,

Government is pleased to offer to you appointment as Senior Adviser in the Cabinet Secretariat, until further orders, on the following terms and conditions:-

i) token pay of Re.1/- per month;

ii) free residential accommodation, as per entitlement or payment of Rs.1000/- per month in lieu thereof;

iii) facility of staff car for official journeys including journeys from office to residence and back;

iv) residential telephone; and

v) entertainment allowance of Rs.500/- per mensum.

2. The appointment will be on contract basis. You will be subject to provisions of the Indian Official Secrets Act, 1923.

3. Kindly convey your acceptance to the above terms.

Yours faithfully,

(R. Parameswar)
Joint Secretary to the Cabinet.

*Working for a salary of Re 1 as senior advisor between 1981 and 1984*

R.N. Kao

SAKETA
E-10/2 Vasant Vihar
New Delhi-110057

August 18, 1999.

My dear Balachandran,

Thank you very much for your letter of the 3rd instant. I regret that there has been some delay on my part in acknowledging it.

I had missed your article which appeared in the Times of India on the 15th of July, but I have now read it with interest.

I think that in several ways, the shortcomings in our present system to which you have referred, arise out of our inheritance from a colonial regime which distrusted the bulk of the people. Consequently, it laid great stress on official secrecy. Since independence, we have had a great churning in our system, but there is need for more of that. What do you think of the announcement yesterday, made by the National Security Adviser about the doctrine which we are going to follow in respect of missiles and nuclear weapons? Was it necessary at this time?

Before closing this letter, may I compliment you on the compelling logic of what you have said in your article and the felicity of your language. Some of the questions which you have raised, had been considered while I was in my second recarnation as Senior Adviser in the Cabinet Secretariat, and the role of the Cabinet Committee for Political Affairs was examined. Unfortunately, we have little institutional memory. Consequently, it seems to me that often we spend a lot of time and effort trying to rediscover the wheel.

With kind regards,

Yours sincerely,

Shri V. Balachandran,
Flat 131, "BUENA VISTA"
Gen. Bhosle Marg,
MUMBAI - 400 021.

---

SAKETA
E-10/2 Vasant Vihar
New Delhi-110057

May 12, 1998.

My dear Balachandran,

Thank you very much for your letter of the 4th instant and its enclosure.

I read with interest your article on the need of intelligence reform, and am impressed with the contents of what you have said. The points which you have made are telling, stressing
(a) that despite the end of the cold war, the importance of intelligence has not diminished, and
(b) that the investment made in setting up a strong intelligence organisation, is much less than the expenditure which would be involved in making adequate military arrangements for the defence of the country.

I agree with your observation that the interest of the elected representatives of the people in knowing more about the work of the intelligence agencies, is legitimate. It would be wise to accept this demand and to cooperate with the elected representatives in a selective manner. This happens in all democracies, and would happen in India too. If one foresees a certain inevitable change, it is wiser to cooperate in the process than to offer stiff resistance, which is bound to be overwhelmed eventually.

With kind regards, and wishing you all the best,

Yours sincerely,

Shri V. Balachandran,
131, Buena Vista,
Gen. Bhosle Marg,
Mumbai - 400 021.

---

R.N. KAO

SAKETA
E-10/2 Vasant Vihar
New Delhi-110057

Dated: September 25, 2000

My dear Balachandran,

I am writing this to compliment you on your article "Intelligible Intelligence", which was published here in the Times of India, dated 21st instant.

The point, which you have mentioned, is very significant. It is not enough either for the IB or the R&AW to send intelligence reports to the Government. Someone with adequate experience, has to interpret these reports to the Government. In 1981, before I was appointed in the Cabinet Secretariat, as Senior Adviser, in briefing me, the late Mrs.Indira Gandhi, had said to me, amongst other things, that the intelligence organisations by themselves, "did not see the wood for the trees". I made a small beginning to remove this deficiency, but, other events intervened, and the whole venture was aborted. Whatever little I was able to accomplish, during my short tenure, in my second incarnation, was possible only because of the Prime Minister's personal support.

I agree with you that Mr. Saxena has a great opportunity to improve things, or at least to make suitable recommendations for improving things.

I hope that things are going well with you and your family, and that you keep yourself usefully busy.

With warm regards,

yours sincerely,

Mr. V. Balachandran
Flat No. 131, Buena Vista
Gen. J. Bhosle Marg
MUMBAI - 400021

---

R.N. KAO

SAKETA
E-10/2 Vasant Vihar
New Delhi-110057

Dated: October 9, 2000

My dear Balachandran,

I acknowledge with thanks the receipt of your letter dated the 25th of September, with which you had sent to me a copy of your article published in the Times of India, on the 21st.

It seems to me that my letter to you on the same subject, crossed yours in the post. Elaborating on what I hinted at in my last letter to you, I regret to say that we appear all the time to be in the process of reinventing the wheel. This results in our failure to build institutions. Luckily, we have so far been able to blunder through in spite of these factors. For the future, I hope that Mr. Saxena's efforts would bear useful fruit. The environment seems to be getting more challenging.

Please accept our congratulations for yourself and your wife, on your elder daughter's engagement to be married to an eligible bridegroom in Dubai. We also send our blessings to her. From all accounts which one hears, Dubai is not a bad place to live in.

I notice that on the cover of your letter, the address of my house is given as E-10/2, Vasant Vihar. In fact, the number is E-10/2. Luckily, I am notorious enough in this locality, so, the post-man brought the letter to me.

It is reassuring to know that you are well. Given the circumstances, we manage to get along in a low key. There are usual pains and aches that flesh is heir to, but, one cannot really complain.

... 2/-

*Kao kept in touch with many of his former colleagues.*
*He had particular fondness for Balachandran as these letters show*

*At one of the R&AW's functions after retirement.*
*To his right, Sankaran Nair*

*The rarely photographed P.N. Banerjee alias Nath Babu (extreme right)*
*with Sheikh Mujib's family in Dhaka.*
*Banerjee's son Soumitra is standing on extreme left*
*Photo courtesy:* Soumitra Banerjee

*A medal of honour given by the Government of Ghana
after Kao passed away*

*With Gary Saxena (centre), one of his worthy successors*

*With former PMs I.K. Gujral (top) and A.B. Vajpayee (below)*

*Kao in his prime*

*Kao with women officers of R&AW. Two of them are still serving*

*With two of his successors, A.S. Dulat (left) and C.D. Sahay (centre)*

*Kao in his 80s*

*Perhaps his last public appearance. Kao with Vikram Sood, the then R&AW chief in December 2001*

# NINE

# The Pressing Need for a Foreign Intelligence Agency

The 22-day war between India and Pakistan in September 1965 is a largely forgotten period of India's politico-military-diplomatic history. It happened in less than four years after the Chinese debacle and immediately after India's first prime minister, Jawaharlal Nehru, had died heartbroken and defeated by what he thought was the Chinese betrayal.

Most popular accounts about the 1965 war have spoken about it being a stalemate, but a more detailed reading and subsequent assessment shows that India not only turned the tables on Pakistan which, at that point in history, had superior military hardware and was backed by major powers. India, on the other hand, was economically weak and was passing through an uncertain political phase following the death of Pandit Nehru and was yet to fully recover from the politico-military-diplomatic humiliation of 1962.

Under the circumstances, Lal Bahadur Shastri's steely resolve, Y.B. Chavan's pragmatic leadership in the defence ministry and the courage and fortitude of the Indian military not only withstood Pakistan's aggression but, in the end, forced Pakistan on the defensive. In pure statistical terms too, Pakistan lost more territory, more tanks and more men in the war.

In *1965: Turning the Tide: How India Won the War*, I wrote the following on the 1965 war—'Looking back, India could have done better by being bolder in the field and by better appreciating the operational and strategic context. It could have, for instance, deployed its navy in an offensive mode but it did not... But this is a judgement in retrospect, 50 years later. At that time, it was the best India as a nation could have done. More importantly, if the Indian military had not gone through the baptism of 1965, it could not have done as spectacularly as it did in 1971 in breaking up Pakistan and help create Bangladesh, a new nation.'[1]

Fifty years after, it is clear that India not only thwarted the Pakistani designs but also inflicted unacceptable losses on the Pakistani military triggering many changes within that country's politico-military structure. Even Ayub's own son, Gauhar Ayub Khan, has admitted that the war should not have taken place. In an interview to *Outlook*, he said, 'It was a war which should not have taken place. It set Pakistan back and was also costly for India. It led from events in Kashmir which Pakistan considered would be contained there and

---

[1] Nitin A. Gokhale, *1965: Turning the Tide: How India Won the War* (New Delhi: Bloomsbury, 2015).

not turn into an open conflict between the two countries. But when India attacked Lahore and other fronts, it led to a general war between India and Pakistan. Ayub Khan was not looking for a war with India.'[2]

An unintended consequence of the 1965 war was the boost that the opposition leaders in East Pakistan (now Bangladesh) received to their demand for more autonomy to the eastern wing. When asked what the security guarantees for the eastern part of undivided Pakistan against an Indian military campaign were, Ayub or his military commanders had no convincing reply. This encouraged Sheikh Mujibur Rahman, leader of the Awami League, to intensify his agitation for greater autonomy for the Bengali-majority East Pakistan that eventually led to the fragmentation of Pakistan and creation of Bangladesh, aided in large measure, no doubt, by India's military might and diplomatic offensive in 1971. The defeat in 1965 also eventually led to Ayub's downfall in 1969.

But if Pakistan suffered internal turmoil in the wake of the 1965 experience, the Indian military and intelligence agencies too experienced many embarrassing moments. There were lasting lessons too, but first the gaffes.

## What India Gained and Lost

Although militarily India clearly had an upper hand at the end of the war, the Indian Army could have done better with a little more dash and imagination on the part of its

---

[2] Interview to *Outlook*.

leaders. Field Commanders lacked a clear objective. They did not know during or before the conflict if the aim of the campaign was for an all-out war, a war for conquest of territory or simply an effort to whittle down Pakistan's war-waging capability. It was only after the conclusion of the war that the top brass is supposed to have mentioned that the 22-day military campaign was intended to be a war of attrition!

Moreover, except for a couple of instances, the performance of India's field commanders left a lot to be desired. For most part, the leadership was too defensive—timid even—in its thinking.

The biggest failure, however, was deemed to be on the intelligence front.

Despite the on-going tension in Kashmir and the Kutch region in which the Pakistani Army caught the Indian defence by surprise in the spring of 1965, Indian intelligence failed to anticipate the massive infiltration planned by Pakistan under Operation Gibraltar. There was also a lack of assessment on how Pakistan may respond to the failure of the operation. Had the intelligence apparatus been effective, India would have anticipated the thrust in Chhamb-Jaurian (Operation Grand Slam). However, by all accounts, everyone was caught by surprise at the magnitude of the Pakistani offensive launched on 1 September. P.V.R. Rao, the then Defence Secretary, observed later, 'The attack by Pakistan at Chhamb on the morning of 1 September came as a surprise in its exact location and intensity of the attack. From 26 August, there were heavy Pakistani troop movement in the area under our continuous observation but the Army had concluded that the attack would come further north.'[3]

The bigger failure, and, perhaps, of a larger strategic import, was India's lack of ability to assess the limits of ammunition available with Pakistan. Despite knowing that the Americans—who were the principal weapons supplier to Pakistan during that time—always gave less than a month's ammunition to its clients. India lacked the intelligence on the shortage of ammunition in the Pakistani arsenal. As it turned out, by 22 September—when ceasefire was declared— Pakistan had practically run out of its stock of ammunition without any replenishment in sight since the Americans had already imposed an arms embargo. Had the war continued for some more time, Pakistan would have collapsed and who knows, the subcontinental history would have taken a different turn.

But that did not happen. But something good came out of the failure of intelligence. India bifurcated the task of collecting external and internal intelligence and created the Research and Analysis Wing (R&AW).

## Kao Gets Another Crucial Task

This is where Ramji Kao was assigned a role that would allow him to leave a lasting impact on many aspects of Indian security and intelligence. He was destined to play a greater role in the making of India's history.

---

[3] Nitin A. Gokhale, *1965: Turning the Tide: How India Won the War* (New Delhi: Bloomsbury, 2015).

Having set up ARC and headed it until 1966, RNK was also the head of external intelligence in the IB. B.N. Mullik, the longest serving Chief of an Indian intelligence organisation, had retired as the director of IB in October 1964, but continued to remain Director General (security), established an office in 1963 to coordinate the national security system and intelligence apparatus. Mullik's successor was S.P. Verma.

But the bigger change had happened at the prime ministerial level. Shastri had died in January 1966 and Indira Gandhi, Nehru's daughter, became India's third Prime Minister.

At that point in time, she was considered a political lightweight and the Congress Party stalwarts, who helped her ascend to the top post, had hoped to control her from the shadows. Within a couple of years, however, she outwitted most of her seniors in the party to rule India for over a decade. She had the ability to pick the right team and then leave implementation of her policies to them. One key appointment she made in 1967 was P.N. Haksar. A Kashmiri Pandit, who had never lived in Kashmir, Haksar, along with RNK, was to play a seminal role in most of Indira Gandhi's momentous decisions between 1967 and 1975. Haksar, in his capacity as secretary to the prime minister, in fact helped RNK to create R&AW.

There are many reasons cited in public domain why R&AW was created. However, in absence of any official document in public domain on the subject, we will never know the exact reasoning given by RNK in a detailed note to Mrs Gandhi in late 1967 or early 1968. That background note is still classified. K. Sankaran Nair, RNK's closest friend and colleague, has, however, written a longish passage in his book as to why and how R&AW came into being.

Nair's contention in his book is based on his personal knowledge and memory. He wrote, 'As often happens with bureaucracy, the right hand does not know what the left hand does. Sometimes it cuts its nose to spite the rivals' face, in the course of turf wars.'[4]

Nair was referring to what he calls a minor conflict that had erupted in 1965 between the army and the Bureau over intelligence turf immediately after the war with Pakistan. Apparently, Army Chief General J.N. Choudhry sent a strong paper to the minister of defence, Y.B. Chavan. His main point was that the Army could not land a decisive blow on Pakistan because precise intelligence was not available since collection of intelligence was entrusted to 'flat-footed Clouseaus of the IB'.[5]

The paper argued that military intelligence should be the preserve of military men who should be posted abroad in Indian missions abroad to collect information, replacing the IB representatives. Defence Minister Chavan agreed with these views but the cabinet did not pursue the matter at that time.

When Mrs Gandhi took over as the prime minister, there were many seniors in her cabinet who had longer administrative

---

[4] K. Sankaran Nair, *Inside IB and RAW: The Rolling Stone that Gathered Moss* (New Delhi: Manas Publications, 2019).

[5] Ibid.

and political experience. To stamp her authority, Mrs Gandhi had to take many steps to rein in many Congress stalwarts. Nair said that one of those leaders who was cut to size by Mrs Gandhi was Chavan, the strongman from Bombay. Chavan had moved from defence to the home ministry in Mrs Gandhi's cabinet. The Ministry of Home Affairs (MHA) was the controlling authority of the IB then, as it is now.

Nair wrote that Indira Gandhi strongly suspected him (Chavan) of conspiring against her and in 1968, she ordered the Department of Personnel, which was in charge of the administration of the superior civil services like the IAS, the IPS, along with its junior minister of state, should be removed from the home ministry and placed under the prime minister. She then moved the Central Bureau of Investigation (CBI), a powerful police organisation for the investigation of corruption, which could and has been also misused to his political opponents, from the home minister to the Prime Minister. She moved on to weaken the IB by stripping it of its foreign posts, which, among other things, collected important military information abroad. Nair added, 'The defence ministry's 1965 paper on the need to separate foreign intelligence which included military intelligence, from the IB which Chavan had supported, was effectively used to strip the IB of this duty. The prospect of posting abroad was an attraction which had brought good IPS officers from the states to the IB. So this separation of foreign intelligence was meant to impair the efficiency of the IB and therefore its utility to Chavan as home minister.'

Incidentally, nearly 20 years later, during Prime Minister V.P. Singh's tenure, the army once again raised the issue of allowing it to run clandestine operations from the Indian diplomatic missions abroad, says B. Raman, a senior R&AW officer. 'After carefully examining the matter, he reiterated the original decision of Indira Gandhi that the army should collect only tactical military intelligence through trans-border sources and should not run any clandestine operation outside the country. However, V.P. Singh removed the restrictions imposed by his predecessors on the depth up to which it could run the trans-border source operations from the Indian territory.'[6]

Nair remembers that Mrs Gandhi commissioned RNK to produce a paper delineating the structure of the new foreign intelligence agency. He added, 'Kao, now a Joint Director in the IB, was rated as a top-notch officer. Having worked as the personal security officer to Pandit Nehru, he was known to the family. Being a Kashmiri Pandit was no disqualification either.'

Prime Minister Indira Gandhi had given him a free hand except for two conditions. Firstly, the new organisation should be a multidisciplinary one and should not draw its higher personnel exclusively from the IPS. Secondly, the top two posts would be filled at the discretion of the prime minister from within the organisation or from outside.

Nair, who many old timers of R&AW describe as RNK's alter ego, wrote, 'Within a few months, Ramji produced his

⁶ B. Raman, *The Kaoboys of R&AW: Down Memory Lane* (United States, Lancer Publications, 2007).

magnum opus, defining the proposed structure of India's CIA. The designation of the personnel was to be in secretariat terms. The Chief was to be a Secretary and the junior ranks were to run down the line to the rank of Under Secretary.[7] Nair claimed that the then Cabinet Secretary, D.S. Joshi, suggested that the organisation be called R&AW in order to camouflage it and be attached as a wing of the Cabinet Secretariat.

Vappala Balachandran, who worked with RNK from 1975 but had a closer association with him in his post-retirement years, says the raison d'être of R&AW was to be different from the Central Police Organisation. 'R&AW was always clear about the need to keep the organisation away from the police culture. I am extremely proud to be an IPS officer but when I joined R&AW and stayed on, I realised why Mrs Gandhi had emphasised to Kao the need to recruit R&AW officers from the market, if necessary. Intelligence collection, especially foreign intelligence collection, is a completely different cup of tea. Unlike the police or the IB, there is no support system abroad. One has to live by one's wit and be as inconspicuous as possible,' said Balachandran, who had several key foreign postings abroad,

B. Raman, one of the rare R&AW officers to have written extensively about the organisation's functioning, its successes as well as failures, notes, 'When the organisation came into being, Indira Gandhi gave it many special dispensations, such as exempting it from the purview of the Union Public Service Commission (UPSC) in matters of recruitment and

---

[7] Ibid.

promotions, powers of sanction of foreign tours, etc. The head of the R&AW wore two hats. As the head of the organisation, he used to send proposals for director recruitment, sanction of posts, foreign travel, etc. to the Cabinet Secretariat. As a Secretary in the Cabinet Secretariat, he had these proposals examined and sanctioned. The idea was that if the R&AW was to be effective as an external intelligence agency, it should not be subjected to the usual red tape. The grant of these special dispensations demanded that the head of the R&AW exercised these powers objectively with a deep sense of responsibility.'[8]

Nair, who had worked very closely with RNK and had, in fact, succeeded him in Ghana, was asked by Kao if he would join him in building a new organisation that Indira Gandhi had sanctioned. He describes the circumstances under which he agreed to join R&AW. 'The Prime Minister had accepted Ramji's paper and asked him to help the new organization which he had started building. He invited me for lunch one day, explained the developments in the matter and said, "Shanks, will you join me in this task? I know the new boss of the IB has denied you your rightful promotion. I've not got an equivalent rank in the organization, but I shall try my best to get it for you." I replied yes. I would love to join you in the pioneering job as a close friend and colleague. To hell with the rank.' It was, perhaps, one of the most important the two old friends and colleagues would have had over lunch. RNK and Nair made a formidable combination and nurtured the R&AW in its formative

---

[8] Ibid.

years to make it one of the best intelligence outfits in the world.

However, from very early of its existence, the R&AW was a victim of bureaucratic apathy and peer jealousy. The MEA and the IB were naturally unhappy with the formation of the R&AW. IB, because of its prized domain in foreign intelligence, was taken away and the MEA felt that the new organisation would impinge upon its exclusive preserve.

Yet, RNK persisted—thanks to his close friendship with Haksar and implicit faith that Mrs Gandhi had showed in him—and had the organisation up and running quickly. But bureaucratic hurdles continued to dog the R&AW.

In February 1969, less than five months after the R&AW was formed, Haksar prevailed over Mrs Gandhi to write a detailed note on file to smoothen R&AW's functioning since it had fallen victim to bureaucratic tussle. Kao had strongly objected to the attempts by bureaucratic juniors who were trying to control and direct R&AW's functioning. RNK was outraged. He took the matter to Haksar who concurred with him on the point that 'no intelligence organisation can function in this fashion,' and that the head of the R&AW needs to have full powers and functional independence from the usual bureaucratic ways.

The note written to the Cabinet Secretary is worth reproducing in full here. 'The functioning and operation of a Foreign Intelligence Operation is an extremely sensitive and delicate matter. I'm convinced that unless the head of the organisation is allowed the necessary power and autonomy, to function as an Additional Secretary under the overall supervision of the Cabinet Secretary himself, the organisation will run into great many difficulties. The head of the Research and Analysis Wing having been appointed as Additional Secretary, it is in the interest of security and efficiency of work that he should function as such with all the powers, including financial powers normally exercised by Additional Secretaries and that the organisation should be treated as an integral part of the Cabinet Secretariat. I see no objections to secretarial designations being given to officers of the Research and Analysis Wing where it is necessary to do so. For dealing with matters relating to the organisation's administration, establishment and finances, a separate administrative cell should be created in the Cabinet Secretariat. However, it should work under the Additional Secretary and should examine establishment and financial proposals made by the Research and Analysis Wing in consultations with its concerned officers. When necessary, it should make its recommendations to the Cabinet Secretary through the Additional Secretary.'[9]

Nair too remembered the initial friction with different departments. 'Foreign desks in the IB were transferred to R&AW from the IB. Hooja, the new IB director, fought tooth and nail to deny us the chattels of office, like buildings, furniture, account staff and good personnel. But along with my good colleague Hassanwalia, we fought back fang and claw and got R&AW firing on all cylinders,' he wrote.[10]

---

[9] Jairam Ramesh, *Intertwined Lives: PN Haksar and Indira Gandhi* (New Delhi: Simon and Schuster, 2018).

[10] K. Sankaran Nair, *Inside IB and RAW* (New Delhi: Manas Publications, 2019).

Operationally, the R&AW indeed got off to a good start, aided initially by all those who used to work on the IB's foreign desk, which now stood transferred to India's new foreign intelligence organisation. The bureaucratic sniping, however, did not cease so easily. As the R&AW expanded, it wanted to establish new stations abroad after careful assessment and analysis.

In June 1970, RNK was forced to write a note to Foreign Secretary T.N. Kaul, drawing his attention to the delay in clearing two proposals sent by the R&AW. The note said, 'Given below are the brief particulars of two proposals, action regarding which has been held up in the MEA: (i) Establishment of new units for external intelligence work in our missions at Paris, Bonn, Istanbul, Hanoi, Phnon Penh, Suva (Fiji), Mauritius and Trinidad; (ii) Creation of a post in the R&AW for liaison work relating to the foreign intelligence requirements of the MEA. The post is to be that of a director, and should be filled by an officer of the IFS whose services may be made available to the R&AW on deputation from the MEA. A similar liaison cell has already been formed in the R&AW for the intelligence requirements of the Defence Services Headquarters. It is headed by a Major General, supported by three officers of the rank of Brigadier and other junior staff.'[11]

The original proposal with detailed justification for establishment of each of these stations and more was given to the MEA in December 1969. RNK wanted 13 stations

---

[11] Opening of new units of the R&AW in our diplomatic missions abroad. P.N. Haksar papers, Subject File No. 227, NMML, New Delhi.

to be established. Kaul, the Foreign Secretary pared the demand down to eight listed above. The MEA was to give its concurrence to the R&AW proposal and forward it to the Finance Ministry for 'necessary financial sanction.'

It is interesting to note how the stations that the R&AW wanted to establish half a century ago continue to be important. In its note, the R&AW had given the following justification for each of them:

1. Paris and Bonn: During the recent years, France has become the major supplier of sophisticated weapons to various countries of Africa and Asia. Pakistan has been trying to equip several squadrons of its Air Force with Mirage aircraft, apart from her attempts to acquire French submarines. There have also been reports of Pakistani negotiations to secure tanks through various European countries including West Germany. This country is also one of the major sources of technical know-how in rocketry and aerodynamics, which China is known to be trying to acquire. It is, therefore, necessary that we should have a presence in Paris and Bonn to be able to obtain information about Pakistani and Chinese efforts in this direction, and other connected developments which concern our security.

2. Istanbul: This port town has become one of the important centres of espionage and counter espionage in Turkey. In the years since the Second World War, Turkey being the common link between

various military alliance, and has acquired a peculiar importance of its own. Much of what happens there is of direct interest to us because of Pakistan's close association with that country. Istanbul is the headquarters of the Turkish cargo lines apart from a number of important defence institutions which are located there, such as the Turkish Defence College, where Pakistani personnel are also sent for training. A good number of Turks visit Pakistan for various purposes from Istanbul. They constitute a rich potential for our work. In view of this, it is of urgent importance that a unit of the R&AW be established at Istanbul under the supervision of a senior officer of this organisation.

3.  Hanoi and Phnon Penh: In South East Asia, North Vietnam and recently Cambodia have come to occupy a position of special importance as being the scene of unfolding Chinese policies in this whole region. We had an officer of the rank of First Secretary at Hanoi until 1962 when the post was abolished. Hanoi being of vital importance in the developments in South East Asia, this capital provides an ideal listening post for us. Therefore, it would be very desirable for us to be able to re-establish our presence in Hanoi at an early date. The importance of Cambodia in the current fast-developing situation of Indo-China is self-evident. In view of our immediate interest in this area, and the need to study Chinese policies and her intentions,

it is necessary to establish a unit of the R&AW in Phnon Penh.

4.  Mauritius, Fiji and Trinidad: Mauritius, particularly after the closure of the Suez, has regained its importance as the 'key to the Indian Ocean'. The MEA are aware of our interest in Mauritius and the security and intelligence agencies operating in this island. Detailed proposal for establishing a unit of the R&AW in our mission in this country has been sent separately to MEA. Fiji provides a strategic position in the Pacific Ocean. Trinidad provides an important listening post for covering developments of relevance to us in the Caribbean Sea and the adjoining parts of South America. We have a vital and growing interest in these three countries. In view of the present demography, there is a large number of people of Indian origin. These units would be used as listening posts as well as jumping boards for launching clandestine operations and servicing them.[12]

Despite the bureaucratic jostling, Kao and Nair were clear that the R&AW needed to have good functional relationship with the two main consumers of foreign intelligence, the MEA and the three service headquarters. In a note dated 7 May 1970, RNK wrote, 'In view of the special importance which the R&AW must attach to the requirements of foreign intelligence of the Ministry of External Affairs, it is felt necessary to establish another special facility in this

---

[12] Ibid.

organization, for carrying out liaison duties in relation to this aspect of our work. The officer in charge of it would be utilised to help transmit to the operational desks in the R&AW, the intelligence needs of the Ministry of External Affairs and the relevant priorities. Simultaneously, he would convert to the Ministry of External Affairs the R&AW's operational considerations, and explain the parameters of its work. This is a very delicate task requiring a full understanding on the one hand of the expertise of foreign intelligence clandestine operations, and on the other, a feel for the political and diplomatic considerations which weigh with the ministry of external affairs.'[13]

He went on to emphasise the importance of posting a director-level officer in the R&AW to function as a link between the MEA and the newly created foreign intelligence organisation. RNK pointed out that a military liaison cell, headed by a Major General, had recently been formed in the R&AW headquarters. 'Its functions are to interpret the requirements of the defence services to the R&AW, and to help fix the targets for military intelligence and their priorities, apart from presenting when necessary, the intelligence furnished by us through the defence services in the correct perspective. This cell will also be utilised for assisting in the training and the briefing of our officers and in diverse other ways, where their special knowledge and experience would be useful.'[14]

---

[13] Ibid.

[14] Ibid.

The spadework, which the new organisation's leadership did in the first couple of years of its existence, was to make a huge difference in its operations in East Pakistan in 1971, prior to the outbreak of hostilities there leading to the subsequent war with Pakistan in December 1971 and the creation of Bangladesh.

# TEN

# Watching the Neighbourhood

In the mid- and late 1960s, after nearly two decades of relative stability post the Second World War, the world was in turmoil again. The student protests in France, the fight for civil liberties in the US, the attempted uprising in Prague and the Woodstock moment, all combined to create uncertainty and chaos in Europe and America, sending ripples everywhere. In India, the Naxalbari rebellion launched by two schoolteachers had caught the imagination of the youth in Bengal and beyond; in neighbouring East Pakistan too, Dhaka University became the hub of revolutionary thought.

East Pakistan's tallest political leader of that time, Sheikh Mujibur Rahman, was stepping up his efforts seeking autonomy for the Bengali-speaking half of Pakistan. Mujib was the rising star behind several popular causes, but chiefly behind the language movement in which the Bengali-speaking population protested against the blanket imposition of Urdu as the main language. The inherent contradictions in the creation of Pakistan were coming to head.

In West Pakistan too—and mainly in its prime cities, Lahore and Karachi—university campuses were boiling over, erupting in protests over several basic shortcomings. Field Marshal Ayub Khan, having ruled Pakistan since 1958 with the full backing of the military, was gradually losing control; Pakistani politicians, led by Zulfikar Ali Bhutto, were on the rise.

Twenty years after the partition of India and the creation of Pakistan, it was clear that except religion, nothing was common between West and East Pakistan. They were not only separated by 1,600 km of Indian territory but also the two wings had completely different cultures, languages, literature and history. At the time of India's Independence, the creation of Pakistan as a Muslim state may have suited the British but right from the beginning, it was an artificial construct. Though politically separated from India, East Pakistan always shared the composite culture of undivided Bengal in history, language, literature, art and music. It had little in common with the people of the western wing. The language was an issue of conflict between the two halves of Pakistan. Bangla was the primary language spoken in the eastern wing. On the other hand, Urdu, Punjabi, Sindhi, Baluchi and Pashto were spoken in the four provinces of West Pakistan.

West Pakistan politicians believed that their country had more in common with the Arab world of West Asia while

East Pakistan was more akin to cultures and climate of South East Asia. East Pakistan, with an area of 139,795 sq. km, had a population of 50.84 million, which was much larger than 42.9 million in West Pakistan, according to the 1961 census. The overall numerical superiority of East Pakistan was, however, nullified unjustly under the principle of parity contained in the constitutions of 1956 and 1962. This was always a major irritant in the relations between the two wings.

West Pakistan was the bastion of landlords, the all-powerful feudals—the Khans, Chaudharis, Mirs and Waderas. In East Pakistan, by contrast, power was vested in the hands of the educated middle class. The influence of the intellectuals, the teachers and the lawyers on the masses was considerable.

Shiekh Mujibur Rahman, who had spent considerable time in politics, initially was an enthusiastic volunteer for the Muslim League and later, was an understudy to Huseyn Shaheed Suhrawardy (the last Chief Minister of undivided Bengal before the Partition and later the Prime Minister of Pakistan in the mid-1950s). As a Bengali, Mujib was at the forefront of the language agitation and gained fame as a vociferous proponent of Bengali as a principle language in East Pakistan. He sought more autonomy for the eastern wing, but all available literature suggests that he was not really in favour of breaking up Pakistan—at least not in the late 1950s and early 1960s. The second Kashmir War of 1965 between India and Pakistan, however, appears to have forced a change in Mujib's outlook.

President Ayub and his foreign minister, Zulfikar Ali Bhutto, initiated the war in the mistaken belief that they had an upper hand against India. As the war raged on the western front, the Eastern part of Pakistan was left defenceless. It was sheer luck and circumstances that prevented the war from spilling over into the eastern wing of Pakistan.

The war remained confined to J&K, Punjab and, to an extent, the Rajasthan border. At the end of the war, however, Bengalis from East Pakistan started asking questions: What if India had attacked this part of Pakistan? Why was there not enough security or deployment of forces in the east? Neither Ayub nor his military commanders had a convincing reply. Some military analysts in Pakistan, in fact, told East Pakistani leaders that they need not worry. The Chinese (who by then had started getting close to Pakistan) would come to their rescue by opening a front against India in the east!

A statement by Bhutto in the national assembly post the 1965 war added fuel to the fire. As Lt Gen A.A.K. Niazi writes in his book, *The Betrayal of East Pakistan*, 'After the 1965 war, Zulfikar Ali Bhutto made a statement in the National Assembly, which caused a furore. He said East Pakistan had been 'saved by China'. This was not a simple statement, but one which had far-reaching consequences. The Bengalis' thinking underwent radical change. It began to appear that if the bulk of the forces are located in West Pakistan, and there were hardly any troops in East Pakistan to defend it, then the Union with Pakistan held no practical advantages. This feeling soon gained strength. The diffident attitude of the West Pakistan leadership failed to justify their strategy. The Bengalis were convinced more than ever before that they were being neglected. To a certain extent their anxieties were not unfounded.'[1]

Apart from these security issues, Mujib and his party, the Awami League, were getting increasingly disillusioned with the treatment meted out to the Bengali half of Pakistan and were determined to fight on politically. Mujib intensified his agitation for greater autonomy for the Bengali-majority East Pakistan.

The 1965 war with India took its toll on Pakistan in more ways than one. Within a couple of years after the war, President Ayub lost all credibility and had to make way for Gen Yahya Khan in 1969, who became the President of Pakistan. Pakistan was brought under martial law in March 1969. In 1970, Yahya Khan ordered elections after agreeing to the principle of 'one man, one vote'—a long-cherished dream of East Pakistanis.

The Awami League, despite its reservations about disproportionate powers vested in the hands of the President to accept or reject the Constitution that would be framed by whichever party came to power after the elections, was all geared up to participate in the elections.

Mujib had consistently advocated a six-point programme for more autonomy to East Pakistan since 1966, and he decided to make that manifesto the cornerstone of his election campaign in 1970 too. The six-point formula he had advanced was as following:

---

[1] Lt Gen A.A.K. Niazi, *Betrayal of East Pakistan* (Pakistan: Oxford, 1998).

1. Parliamentary democracy and genuine federal constitution
2.  Limiting powers of the central government to just two subjects: defence and foreign affairs
3. Separate currencies for East and West Pakistan
4. To maintain independent foreign exchange deposits for each wing
5. Separate fiscal policy for each wing
6. To maintain separate military/militia force for each wing

This formula was, however, unacceptable to the deep establishment in West Pakistan, and Mujib always knew he had an uphill task getting even part of his agenda fulfilled. He pressed on regardless, fully aware that he had the majority of the Bengalis in East Pakistan behind him.

As 1970 rolled on, the Martial Law administration under Gen Yahya Khan (he had replaced Ayub in 1969) decided to hold the elections on 7 December 1970 after postponing it once. As bad luck would have it, less than a month before elections were to be held, East Pakistan was battered by a devastating cyclone on 12 November 1970. It killed close to one million people.

In a humanitarian gesture, India announced a major grant of 50 million rupees and sent hundreds of trucks loaded with essential items. Awami League volunteers also chipped in wherever they could. The party's election campaign was impacted positively by this timely help. The response from West Pakistan, especially from Yahya's administration, was indifferent. This casual approach fuelled the latent anger among the Bengalis against West Pakistan.

The elections were largely free and fair, and Awami League in East Pakistan and Bhutto's Pakistan People's Party (PPP) were riding on popular but different waves. Yet, no one could have imagined the outcome. The PPP won a modest 83 seats out of 144 seats of the National Assembly (equivalent to India's Parliament) in West Pakistan; the Awami League, in contrast, swept the polls in the East bagging 167 of the 169 seats!

This unexpected outcome meant that the military regime would now have to take the Awami League's six-point demand seriously. Even more sinister for the West Pakistanis, the Awami League had a chance to rule entire Pakistan on the strength of its majority of 167 seats in a House of 313. No other party, not even the PPP, came close to the Awami League's numbers. Under normal circumstances, Sheikh Mujibur Rahman was all set to become the prime minister of Pakistan.

But circumstances were not normal. The ruling elite in West Pakistan, including the all-powerful military dictator, Gen Yahya Khan, was not willing to hand over power to those who they saw as their poor, second-class cousins. Yahya and his advisers started looking for ways to deny Mujib and his party the legitimate prize. So various alternatives were thought of. The first option was to let Mujib and his party frame the Constitution that could then be rejected by the President and allow Gen Yahya to continue. The second option was to persuade Mujib and Bhutto to enter into a coalition government and set them off against each other. The third was to maintain status quo, although the last option was fraught with consequences and loss of face for Yahya who had promised transfer of power to the elected representatives.

The game plan started unfolding rapidly. Firstly, Yahya Khan sent congratulatory messages to both Mujib and Bhutto which in itself was questionable since Mujib had clearly won the elections and, therefore, had the mandate to be the prime minister. As if on cue, a few days later, Bhutto declared that the authority at the centre needed to be shared between Awami League and PPP, since the Awami League had not won a single seat in the western part of the country!

The deadlock continued even as Yahya Khan travelled to Dhaka on 12 January 1971 to confer with Mujib. Playing to the gallery during a press conference there, he described Mujib as the future prime minister of Pakistan and that he would soon be handing over the reins of power to 'Sheikh Sahib'.

## R&AW Comes into Play

India was watching the events unfolding in Pakistan closely. The R&AW, tasked with foreign intelligence, was keeping a wary eye on India's neighbour. In a 25-page secret note dated 14 January 1971 (two days after Yahya had landed in Dhaka), addressed to the Cabinet Secretary (with a copy to P.N. Haksar), RNK warned of the possibility of Pakistan launching a military campaign against India to divert attention.[2]

---

[2] Threat of a military attack or infiltration campaign by Pakistan (R&AW note to Cabinet Secretary), Subject file No. 220, P.N. Haksar papers (III Instalment), NMML, New Delhi.

He went on to elaborate, 'After the recent elections, Sheikh Mujibur Rahman has emerged as the unchallenged leader of East Pakistan... He would, therefore, be in a strong position to press for the incorporation of his party's six-point programme in the Constitution. He would find it difficult to make any compromise in his stand on the main Constitutional issues, since his party had declared that the elections would be considered as a referendum on the six-point programme.'[3]

The R&AW note pointed out that 'In the Western Wing of Pakistan, particularly the Punjab and Sindh [Zulfikar Ali], Bhutto seems to have captured the imagination of the common man, because of his promises of early radical changes in the social and economic order... It is difficult to judge whether his anti-India posture yielded him rich dividends, because other rightist parties, the leaders of which also consistently indulged in India-baiting, did badly in the elections.'[4]

In RNK's assessment, the peculiar situation that had emerged in Pakistan after the election results presented a big dilemma for President Yahya Khan. He noted, 'The present ruling elite consisting of hard-liners in the Armed Forces, the privileged bureaucrats and the vested economic and federal interests might possibly exert pressure on Yahya Khan to try to reserve the trend towards the transfer of power to the representatives of the people in the circumstances which have emerged from the elections. In that event, there would be a temptation for Yahya Khan to consider the prospects of embarking on a military venture against India with a view to

---

[3] Ibid.
[4] Ibid.

diverting the attention of the people from the internal political problems and justifying the continuance of the Martial Law.'[5]

The situation in Pakistan remained fluid and Yahya was trying to find a political solution through a compromise between Mujib and Bhutto. However, RNK, whose job was to look at the worst-case scenarios, concluded, '[The] present political situation in Pakistan has not crystallised and is at a very crucial stage. The success or failure of the current Constitutional experiment could be expected to have a definite impact on Pakistan's policy towards India. If the present Martial Law regime sincerely desires to bring about political stability in the country and pacify the alienated East Pakistani with a view to keeping the two Wings together, it would avoid a military show down with India. The threat of a military attack or infiltration campaign by Pakistan would also recede if genuine democracy starts functioning in Pakistan. There would, however, be increased possibility of Pakistan resorting to a military venture against India if the democratic process is aborted or the National Assembly is dissolved either due to its failure to evolve an agreed Constitution or refusal by Yahya Khan to authenticate it.'[6]

The R&AW note had also estimated the Pakistani military strength at that point in time and had concluded, 'Pakistan has considerably increased her armed strength since 1965. Her Army, Navy and Air Force have achieved a good state of military preparedness for any confrontation with India. The potential threat of a military attack by Pakistan on India is

---

[5] Ibid.
[6] Ibid.

quite real, particularly in view of the Sino-Pakistan collusion. Pakistan has also the capability of launching another infiltration campaign into Jammu & Pakistan.'[7]

The note concluded that the Sino-Pakistan collusion was on the rise but correctly predicted—as it was proved in December 1971—that in the event of a military conflict between India and Pakistan, China will not directly intervene but will support Pakistan morally and materially. 'The relations between China and Pakistan continue to be close… However, while there have been clear indications of collusion between China and Pakistan in pursuing an antagonistic policy towards India, there is little evidence so far to show that these two countries are planning a concerted military action against India… It is unlikely that China would actively get involved, militarily, in Indo-Pakistan conflict. Nevertheless, it is to be expected that in the event of all out hostilities between India and Pakistan, China would adopt a threatening posture on the Sino-Indian border and even stage some border incidents and clashes, to prevent the diversion of Indian troops, assigned to meet the Chinese threat, to the theatres of war with Pakistan. China would also assist Pakistan by arranging a steady flow of supplies and military stores.'[8]

The R&AW had assessed that Pakistan had persistently procured military hardware from all available sources. This hardware had been utilised to build the strength and equipment of Pakistani armed forces and the stockpile of reserves. The US had also offered to sell to Pakistan 300

---

[7] From Internal correspondence.
[8] Ibid.

armoured personnel carriers, seven B-57 bombers, six F-104 star fighters and four P-3 Orion long range maritime reconnaissance aircraft. Pakistan and France had concluded negotiations on procuring 24 Mirage III E and 30 Mirage V aircraft over the next two-three years, the R&AW informed Prime Minister Indira Gandhi. India, on the other hand, was erratic in modernising its military after the 1965 war.

RNK's note pointed towards Pakistan's likely attempts to increase infiltration of small groups of armed and well-trained personnel into J&K. 'The main targets of the infiltrators would be bridges, lines of communication, petrol and supply dumps, airfields, formations headquarters, ammunition depots, police stations, power houses and other key installations. It would appear to be the current strategy of Pakistan to work towards building up popular unrest in J&K, which could be exploited at an opportune moment for launching a "liberation movement" there,' the assessment concluded.[9]

Meanwhile, as East Pakistan careened towards an unprecedented crisis, Indian decision makers were already making contingency plans. Prime Minister Indira Gandhi, despite her preoccupation with the upcoming elections, found time to be briefed regularly on the developing situation in East Pakistan. Haksar, her sounding board and principal trouble-shooter, along with RNK was worried about the fallout of the internal trouble in Pakistan.

Hence, based on RNK's 14 January 1971 note about Pakistan's attempts to strengthen her armed forces and create

---

[9] Indian intelligence assessment.

trouble in J&K, Haksar sent a telegram to India's Ambassador to Moscow, detailing the military equipment that India needed urgently to be ready to face any Pakistani aggression. The list included tanks, APCs, guns, ammunition, bomber aircraft, surface-to-air guided weapons and aircraft for India's aircraft carrier. 'We have no, repeat, no other source of supply than to rely upon Soviet readiness to understand and respond to our needs,' Haksar's telegram, quoted by Jairam Ramesh in his 2018 book, said.[10]

Simultaneously, Haksar sought and secured Indira Gandhi's permission to set up a 5-member committee (Committee on East Pakistan), including himself and Kao, under the Cabinet Secretary's chairmanship. It included, the Home Secretary and the Foreign Secretary in the beginning. The committee was formed to figure out ways to respond to the evolving situation in East Pakistan. The work was to be coordinated by RNK as the member secretary showing the importance which he had in the government structure at that point in time. Haksar's note is worth reproducing in full. It asked the following questions:

- What would be the implications, internal as well as external, of India giving recognition to an independent Bangladesh?
- If India gives aid to Bangladesh, what would be various implications under the heads given below:
  These may be considered under two sets of circumstances, viz., with and without formal recognition of Bangladesh:

---

[10] Jairam Ramesh, *Intertwined Lives: PN Haksar and Indira Gandhi* (New Delhi: Simon & Schuster India, 2018).

Implications to be examined

(a) *Political*—both internal and external implications should be considered.

(b) *Economic*—The implications of the economic aid should be examined with reference to India's foreign trade, the possible trans-border trade into Bangladesh and all other relevant factors including the estimate of the cost likely to be entailed in giving such aid.

*Note:* The requirements of Bangladesh include the following:

1. Arms and ammunition (including LMGs, MMGs and mortars)

2. Food supplies amounting to three million tonnes of food stuff

3. Medicines

4. Communications and signals equipment

5. Transport for quick movement inside India around the borders of Bangladesh. The transport includes a small passenger aircraft plus a helicopter

6. Radio transmitter with facilities for Bangladesh broadcast

(c) *Military*—This assessment should include the question whether West Pakistan would retaliate against India particularly in Kashmir. Also, whether there would be any military reaction on the part of China as a close ally of Pakistan.[11]

---

[11] 'PM's instructions about assessment of East Pakistan Affairs' R&AW note for P.N. Haksar, Subject File No. 220, Haksar papers, NMML, New Delhi.

Meanwhile, the R&AW had already activated its sources in East Pakistan.

## P.N. Banerjee alias Nath Babu

Although most Indian diplomats posted in East Pakistan had good contacts with the Awami League, there was one man who had better access than most—PN Banerjee alias 'Nath Babu'. An IPS officer of the West Bengal cadre, Phanishwar Nath (P.N.) Banerjee worked in various districts of the state, did a stint in the State's Special Branch before becoming Superintendent of Police of Tripura. In 1962, he was deputed to the IB.

After a tenure as Deputy Director at the IB headquarters in Delhi between 1962 and 1965, Banerjee was sent back to Calcutta as the man in-charge of the IB's Eastern India office on promotion as the Joint Director (JD). At this point, his career flourished as Banerjee showed exemplary leadership and a penchant for intelligence work.

In 1968, he was made the Joint Secretary in-charge of R&AW's Calcutta station, even as he continued to remain JD, Subsidiary Intelligence Bureau (SIB), Calcutta.

Banerjee's appointment as the JS in R&AW turned out to be a masterstroke. Entrusted by RNK the delicate job of befriending Mujib, Banerjee assumed a new name, P. Nath and a new passport in this new identity. P. Nath incidentally was derived from his first name Phanishwar Nath!

So P. Nath contacted Mujib through some of his friends in East Pakistan and met him for the first time in London in

1968. Thus, began a friendship that lasted until Nath Babu, as Banerjee had come to be known in East Pakistan, passed away suddenly on 24 July 1974 in Dhaka's Inter-Continental Hotel. In that brief period of six years, Nath Babu was RNK's eyes and ears, not just in eastern India but in East Pakistan, Myanmar, Singapore, Thailand and Japan.

His son, Soumitra 'Bobby' Banerjee, a former journalist in Calcutta—and at one time the author's boss in *The Telegraph,* some quarter century ago—reminisces, 'My father became very close to Mujib as they met a number of times in London and other cities across the world in the period between 1968 and 1970. Mujib trusted him totally. I remember when our entire family was invited to Dhaka in March 1972 (after the liberation of Bangladesh), and we went to Mujib's house, he turned to me and said, "you know I trust your father totally. He is the only non-family member to have unrestricted access to my house."'[12] Nath Babu's unfettered access to Mujib and the Awami League leadership helped India get real time and actionable intelligence out of East Pakistan and helped RNK and the Government of India make realistic plans when the balloon went up in March 1971!

As the political crisis deteriorated in February–March 1971, Nath Babu became the most important conduit between Mujib and the Indian Government. He was directly reporting to RNK and Sankaran Nair in Delhi. His updates were keeping the headquarters busy and giving Kao sleepless nights. The inputs were grim. Banerjee's assessment said that

---

[12] Personal interview with Soumitra Banerjee, September 2019.

Pakistan was preparing for a crackdown and it was Kao's job to warn Prime Minister Indira Gandhi and her advisers for a worst-case scenario.

In early March 1971, Mujib had also read the writing on the wall and Yahya's intention not to honour his commitment. He sent a message to Indira Gandhi seeking material and moral help in keeping the Pakistani army at bay. In a message conveyed through Banerjee, Mujib wanted India to give an assurance that it would help East Pakistan. He specifically pointed out that India could 'intercept Pakistani troops, ships and aircraft on the pretext that Pakistan had violated Indian borders.' Mujib felt that Yahya was emboldened to reinforce deployment in East Pakistan because India had withdrawn troops from West Pakistan border.

In reality, Yahya had used an incident of hijacking of an Indian Airlines flight to Lahore on 30 January 1971 as a pretext to beef up security in both East and West Pakistan. The Indian Airlines aircraft was flying from Srinagar to Jammu but was hijacked to Lahore by two members of the Jammu and Kashmir Liberation Front (JKLF), which was fighting for Kashmir's independence. The hijackers were welcomed openly in Pakistan, exacerbating tension with India. While the two hijackers got asylum in Pakistan, India retaliated by suspending Pakistani flights over Indian territory adding to Pakistan's discomfort.

It was against this backdrop that India was weighing its options on East Pakistan. When New Delhi failed to respond immediately to Mujib's request of early March for help, he sent one more message which reached Indira Gandhi on

19 March. India's deputy High Commissioner in Dhaka, K.C. Sen Gupta, carried New Delhi's response. Author and historian, Srinath Raghavan, says Sengupta conveyed to Tajuddin Ahmad, one of Mujib's associates, New Delhi's vague and general assurance that India would offer all possible assistance to victims in the event of an attack.[13] India was not fully committing itself yet, since the Indian leadership was still unsure about the direction in which the events in East Pakistan were headed.

---

[13] Srinath Raghavan, *1971: A Global History of the Creation of Bangladesh* (Ranikhet: Permanent Black, 2013).

# ELEVEN

# The Crackdown in East Pakistan

Even in West Pakistan, there was a sense of uncertainty as Yahya Khan returned to Rawalpindi from Dhaka in mid-January. Yahya's dilemma was understandable. Mujib was in no mood to give up his six-point programme. Bhutto, on the other hand, was egged on by his supporters to claim political primacy.

Meanwhile, the Awami League was getting restless. Yahya Khan, under pressure from Mujib, announced on 13 February 1971 that the National Assembly would meet in Dhaka on 3 March for framing the Constitution. Bhutto, in the meantime, was being encouraged to play spoilsport. On 15 February, Bhutto announced his party's boycott of the National Assembly. He told his followers, 'We cannot go there [Dhaka] only to endorse the Constitution already prepared by a party, and return humiliated.' He told followers at Lahore that he would launch a protest movement if the government backed Mujib. He said either East Pakistan should be allowed independence or Mujib should be arrested and taken to task.

In Dhaka, the situation was grim. Supporters of the Awami League were on a tight leash but beneath the surface, the resentment at the blatant discrimination by Yahya Khan had begun to rankle. The Governor at Dhaka, Vice Admiral S.M. Ahsan and his Martial Law Administrator Lt Gen Shaibzada Yakub, briefed Yahya of the dangerous situation in East Pakistan and advised immediate political action to end the crisis.

As troop build-up was taking place, Governor Ahsan told Mujib of the decision to postpone the National Assembly on 27 February—two days before the public announcement by Yahya on 1 March. He cited two main reasons for postponement—the threat of boycott by Bhutto's PPP and a tense situation created by India on the border. The second reason was a red herring since India had neither moved additional troops to the border nor had it commented on what it considered as an internal affair of Pakistan.

As soon as the announcement was made at noon, streets in Dhaka were flooded with protesting people and the Awami League cadre. In a spontaneous outpouring, common citizens brandishing lathis and iron rods and chanting pro-independence slogans thronged the area around Hotel Purbani, where Mujib and the top brass of the Awami League had gathered to decide the next course of action.

Hours later, Mujib addressed a heavily crowded press conference and criticised the government's decision but stopped short of declaring unilateral independence as many had anticipated. East Pakistan came to a standstill 1 March evening onwards. Next day, Dhaka was strewn with roadblocks put up by angry and almost out-of-control young cadres of the Awami League, and even ordinary citizens who had nothing to do with politics. The anger against blatant discrimination—indeed denial of their fundamental rights, so to speak—had boiled over amongst the East Pakistanis, who considered themselves Bengalis first and Muslims later.

East Pakistan saw a total bandh on 2 March. Mujib was apparently conscious of not letting the agitation turn too violent or going completely out of control. He had to maintain a balance between appearing to be reasonable (to the Pakistani ruling establishment) and inspiring his supporters who were in a heightened mode of protest. Hence, during a speech on 3 March, Mujib appealed to his supporters to observe peaceful satyagraha. He was aware of the palpable anger against the Urdu-speaking 'Bihari' Muslims—people who had moved from India at the time of partition and were seen as outsiders by Bengali-speaking natives—for supporting the ruling elite in East Pakistan. These Urdu-speaking people became an immediate and convenient target of street violence that unleashed in the aftermath of the civil disobedience declared by Mujib on 4 March.

That day onwards, the situation in East Pakistan went into a tailspin. The radicals were disappointed with Mujib's balancing act and decided to chalk their own programme.

Yahya, alarmed at the deteriorating situation, broadcast a speech squarely blaming Mujib for the deadlock. While announcing 25 March as the date for the meeting of the National Assembly, he asserted that 'it is the duty of the Pakistan Armed Forces to ensure the integrity, solidarity and security of Pakistan, a duty in which they have never failed'. Separately, Yahya sent a message to Mujib in attempt of a last-minute reconciliation. At the same time, he sent Lt Gen Tikka Khan to take over from Shahbzada Yakub Khan as Martial Law Administrator and Governor of East Pakistan.

The speech on 7 March is considered a turning point in the political history of East Pakistan/Bangladesh. That day, Sheikh Mujib virtually took control of the administration in the eastern wing of what was then Pakistan. Flags of Independent Bangladesh were seen fluttering at the venue of his meeting that day. As one writer describes it, 'Mujib, in addition to the four conditions laid down by Awami League earlier, also demanded cessation of military buildup in East Pakistan, end to victimisation of government officers and employees and handing over of the maintenance of law and order to police and the East Pakistan Rifles (EPR). Yahya Khan, instead of coming to Dhaka on 10 March, postponed his visit to 15 March and to this Mujib reacted adversely.'[1]

On 16 March, Yahya arrived in Dhaka in what appeared to be a last-ditch effort to clinch a negotiated settlement. At the same time, some generals also arrived in East Pakistan, which, it later transpired, was in preparation for a pre-determined military crackdown. Gen Tikka Khan told President Yahya Khan, 'Give me one week's time, I will bring back normalcy

---

[1] Srinath Raghavan, *1971: A Global History of the Creation of Bangladesh* (Ranikhet: Permanent Black, 2013).

in East Pakistan.' The stage was thus set for a crackdown. A brutal operation, which even seasoned military veterans like Gen Niazi found unpalatable, was about to be unleashed on the unsuspecting people of East Pakistan.

Many accounts of the time now suggest that the die was cast on 18 March when Yahya told Tikka Khan 'the bastard (Mujib) is not behaving. Get ready'.[2]

Meanwhile, in preparation for the crackdown, Gen Tikka ordered eviction of all foreign correspondents and TV crews. Some of them were manhandled, their luggage searched and films removed. Eventually, they all moved to India.

On 25 March, when it was almost certain that a crackdown was coming, Tikka Khan had available to him the four brigades under the 14 Division. As events unfolded on the night of 25 March 1971, neither tact nor tactics was applied. Instead, a massacre of unarmed civilians—student leaders, intellectuals from Dhaka University, poor supporters of the Awami League living in ghettos (most of them were Hindus) and soldiers of the EPR—was unleashed on the unsuspecting population. The dreadful operation dubbed 'Operation Searchlight', which commenced around 11 PM on 25 March, killed anywhere between 7,000 to 10,000 people that night in Dhaka alone, according to independent sources, diplomats and foreign journalist, who were in Dhaka.

It was a complete military operation—one of the very few military operations in post-Second World War history, which ultimately was planned against civilians just to kill a

----

[2] A.A.K. Niazi, *The Betrayal of East Pakistan* (Pakistan: Oxford, 1998).

small percentage of them and to scare the survivors. Many historians have traced the desire for full independence by the Bengali population to events of that horrific night.

The morning of 25 March was tense, as reports of the breakdown of talks and total collapse of the administration led to the death of more than a thousand people in Syedpur, Rangpur, Khalishpur and Chittagong the day before.

Operation Searchlight began at around 11 PM, but the tanks rolled out of the Dhaka cantonment around 8 PM. Some went towards Dhaka University, some to the EPR headquarters in Pilkhana and others towards Rajarbagh Police Lines.

The first target in Dhaka University was the Iqbal Hall (now Sergeant Zahurul Huq Hall), where most of the Bengali nationalist activities took place. To clear their way, the Pakistani Army set fire to the slums, which straddled the old railway line that ran west of Dhaka University and killed thousands of poor men, women and children within a few minutes.

The army also killed a number of teachers that night inside their houses. Dr Moniruzzaman, head of the Department of Statistics, was killed along with his entire family. So was Dr Jyotirmoy Guha Thakurta, reader of English, and Govinda Chandra Dev, head of the Department of Philosophy.

The Army was on a rampage, killing, pillaging virtually unopposed. The Hindu population of Dhaka took the brunt of the slaughter. Dhaka University was targeted, and Hindu students were gunned down. As the news of the military action reached Mujib (who was still at his Dhanmondi residence), he instructed all his top colleagues to go underground. Some student leaders who were meeting Mujib at that time urged him to go ahead and declare independence and call upon the EPR, Police and East Bengal Rifles (EBR). Mujib agreed and around midnight tried to contact the Dhaka Radio Station but the army had already seized it.

He then contacted the Chittagong Radio Station over the EPR wireless to broadcast the declaration of independence. Around midnight, in the first few hours of the massacre, Mujib's voice was heard over the air waves, thanks to the broadcast by the Chittagong Radio Station. The voice, faint, as if pre-recorded, said, 'This may be my last message. From today, Bangladesh is independent. I call upon the people of Bangladesh, wherever you are and with whatever you have to resist the army occupation to the last. Your fight must go on until the last soldier of the Pakistan occupation army is expelled from the soil of Bangladesh and final victory is achieved.'

Mujib was arrested shortly after declaring Bangladesh independent. The rest of the Awami League leadership went into hiding and those that survived eventually fled to India.

For the first few days after the Pakistani Army crackdown, the world, at large, was unaware of the massacre of 25 March and thereafter. Yahya Khan and the Pakistan Army had planned the genocide well. Yahya aimed to crush the Bengali spirit once and for all. Only handful of journalists managed to evade the Pakistani Army.

One of them was Simon Dring of *The Daily Telegraph*. He evaded capture by hiding on the roof of the Hotel Intercontinental. Dring was able to extensively tour Dhaka the next day and personally witness the slaughter that was taking place. Days later, Dring was able to leave East Pakistan with his reporter's notes. On 30 March 1971, he filed a chilling report of the massacre that took place in Dhaka on the night of 25 March. Dring reported that in 24 hours of killing, the Pakistan army slaughtered as many as 7,000 people in Dhaka and up to 15,000 people in all of Bangladesh.

Dring described the attack on Dhaka University as follows:

> *Led by American-supplied M-24 World War II tanks, one column of troops sped to Dacca University shortly after midnight. Troops took over the British Council library and used it as a fire base from which to shell nearby dormitory areas.*
>
> *Caught completely by surprise, some 200 students were killed in Iqbal Hall, headquarters of the militantly anti-government students' union, I was told. Two days later, bodies were still smouldering in burnt-out rooms, others were scattered outside, more floated in a nearby lake, an art student lay sprawled across his easel.*
>
> *Army patrols also razed nearby market area. Two days later, when it was possible to get out and see all this, some of the market's stall-owners were still lying as though asleep, their blankets pulled up over their shoulders.*
>
> *The 'old town' quarter of Dhaka city was singled out for destruction by the Pakistanis because of strong Awami League support there and because there were many Hindu residents in the area.*

Here is how Simon Dring described the attacks on unarmed civilians:

> *The lead unit was followed by soldiers carrying cans of gasoline. Those who tried to escape were shot. Those who stayed were burnt alive. About 700 men, women and children died there that day between noon and 2 pm, I was told.*
>
> *In the Hindu area of the old town, the soldiers reportedly made the people come out of their houses and shot them in groups. The area, too, was eventually razed.*
>
> *The troops stayed on in force in the old city until about 11 pm on the night of Friday, 26 March, driving around with local Bengali informers. The soldiers would fire a flare and the informer would point out the houses of Awami League supporters. The house would then be destroyed—either with direct fire from tanks or recoilless rifles or with a can of gasoline, witnesses said.*

After having massacred 15,000 unarmed civilians in a single day, the Pakistani soldiers bragged about their invincibility to Simon Dring: 'These bugger men', said one Punjabi lieutenant 'could not kill us if they tried'. 'Things are much better now', said another officer. 'Nobody can speak out or come out. If they do, we will kill them—they have spoken enough—they are traitors, and we are not. We are fighting in the name of God and a united Pakistan.

On 27 March, when the curfew was lifted after 33 hours, almost the entire population of Dhaka had started fleeing. Reports of the time said almost 80 per cent of the population had left the city. The people killed in and around Dhaka in those two days of frenzy were estimated to be close to 150,000. Bengali officers and men in EBR and EPR within the Dhaka area were killed.

The Pakistanis then began their killing spree in the major cities of Dhaka, Chittagong, Jessore and Comilla. In Jessore and Comilla Cantonments, Bengali officers (almost 30 each) were killed along with their families. The Pakistan Air Force (PAF) was pressed into service to strafe pockets of resistance. More than 15,000 villages and towns were bombed from air. Non-Bengali collaborators assisted Pakistani soldiers in identifying and locating prominent Hindu and Bengali intellectuals and hunted them down mercilessly. Although the exact figures will never be known, conservative estimates of the time suggest that over a million people were butchered in the barbaric campaign of the Pakistani Army.

In June, the Pulitzer Prize-winning journalist Sydney Schanberg filed a number of eyewitness accounts from Bangladeshi towns for *The New York Times*. In response, the Pakistani Army expelled him from the country on 30 June 1971.

Schanberg described the systematic subjugation and killing of Bengalis as follows:

*Army trucks roll through the half-deserted streets of the capital of East Pakistan these days, carrying 'anti-state' prisoners to work-sites for hard labor. Their heads are shaved and they wear no shoes and no clothes except for shorts—all making escape difficult.*

*Street designations are being changed to remove all Hindu names as well as those of Bengali Moslem nationalists as part of a campaign to stamp out Bengali culture. Shankari Bazar Road in Dacca is now Tikka Khan Road, after the lieutenant general governor of East Pakistan and whom most Bengalis call 'the Butcher'.*

*Since the offensive began the troops have killed countless thousands of Bengalis—foreign diplomats estimate at least 200,000 to 250,000—many in massacres. Although the targets were Bengali Moslems and the 10 million Hindus at first, the army is now concentrating on Hindus in what foreign observers characterize as a holy war.*

*Of the more than six million Bengalis who are believed to have fled to India to escape the army's terror, at least four million are Hindus. The troops are still killing Hindus and burning and looting their villages.*

*However, army commanders in the field in East Pakistan privately admit to a policy of stamping out Bengali culture, both Muslim and Hindu—but particularly Hindu.*

While the world was slow to realise the horrors of the 25–26 March genocide unleashed by the Pakistani Army in East Pakistan, India was alive to the magnitude of the crisis, since lakhs of refugees started streaming into the bordering states of Assam, West Bengal, Tripura and Meghalaya, putting tremendous strain on local resources, and, of course, creating unprecedented social tension.

As soon as the news of the massacres in East Pakistan was public, Indian political parties demonstrated before the Pakistan High Commission in Delhi, demanding immediate withdrawal of the Pakistani Army since it was committing unspeakable atrocities in East Pakistan. On 31 March, the Indian Parliament passed a unanimous resolution expressing grave concern and deep anguish at the massive attack unleashed by the forces of West Pakistan on the people of East Pakistan.

A tsunami of refugees from East Pakistan had hit India's border states. A week after the crackdown in East Bengal, less than 300 refugees had trickled into India. However, in the next fortnight, over 100,000 people crossed over into the Indian states along the border. The figure swelled to over 4,300,000 by May end and to a staggering 7,232,000 by July end and then to a mammoth 10 million!

In New Delhi, the Indian Government was alarmed and harassed. Feeding millions of refugees and managing the logistics was a headache but the bigger challenge was to handle different Awami League leaders who had staggered into India at different times travelling incognito for days.

Tajuddin Ahmad and Amirul Islam, two prominent Awami League leaders, reached the Indian border on 31 March. Srinath Raghavan, who interviewed Amirul Islam years later, writes: 'On the evening of 31 March 1971, having travelled incognito for five days on horseback and foot. Tajuddin Ahmad and Amirul Islam sat anxiously at a culvert in the no-man's land near an Indian border outpost. Their messenger had gone across to establish contact but had not yet returned. Tajuddin was pensive, but Islam felt strangely energised. 'The sun is setting,' he said to Tajuddin, 'but there will be a new dawn' As night fell, they heard the thud of the boots heading in their direction. A small group of soldiers stood before them, presented arms, and welcomed them to India.'[3]

Once in India, escorted by men of Border Security Force (BSF), Tajuddin and Amirul were taken to Calcutta where the then Director General of BSF, K.F. Rustamji, met them and discussed the situation in East Pakistan in detail. The next day, the Awami League leaders were flown to Delhi in preparation to meet Prime Minister Indira Gandhi.

The leaders had realised that to wage a fight for liberation in East Pakistan, they needed to have an organisation and, perhaps, even a provisional government. Bengalis in different parts of the world—including those working in different Pakistani missions across the world—were willing to support the struggle for independence, but a recognised central authority was needed to lend that support. Inaddition, leaders like Tajuddin were worried that if they met the Indian leadership merely as representatives of the Awami League, Delhi would offer a sympathetic ear but would have held back from offering any substantial material support or even military backing in any war of liberation.

So on 10 April 1971, elected representatives from East Pakistan, who had made their way into India in different groups, came on one platform and under the leadership of Tajuddin Ahmad, resolved to set up the provisional

[3] Ibid.

Government of Bangladesh in order to carry out the massive mandate given by the people.

Their proclamation stated, 'We the elected representatives of the people of Bangladesh, whose will is supreme, duly constituted ourselves into a constituent assembly, and having held mutual consultations, and in order to ensure for the people of Bangladesh equality, human dignity and social justice, declare and constitute Bangladesh to be a sovereign people's republic and thereby confirm the declaration of independence already made by Bangabandhu Sheikh Mujibur Rahman and confirm and resolve that till such time as a constitution is framed, Bangabandhu Sheikh Mujibur Rahman shall be the President of the Republic and that Syed Nazrul Islam shall be the Vice-President of the Republic....' In the interim period, till a constitution was framed, the President was to exercise all the executive and legislative powers, and 'do all other things that may be necessary to give to the people of Bangladesh an orderly and just government'. In the absence of the President, the Vice-President would exercise all his powers, duties and responsibilities. The proclamation also went on to say that, 'we further resolve that we undertake to observer and give effect to all duties and obligations devolved upon us as a member of the family of nations and by the charter of the United Nations; we further resolve that this proclamation of Independence shall be deemed to have come into effect since the 26th Day of March 1971.'[4]

---

[4] S.N. Prasad, *The India-Pakistan War of 1971: A History* (Dehradun: Natraj Publishers, 2014).

The proclamation came a week after Tajuddin and other top leaders had met Indira Gandhi in Delhi. No one was clear whether he presented himself as the prime minister of the government-in-exile but the Indian Government knew that after Mujib's arrest, he was effectively the man in-charge of the provisional government.

The formal installation of the Provisional Government of Bangladesh took place on 17 April at Bhaberpura village in the Kustia district of East Bengal near the India-East Pakistan border. A small hamlet—Baidyanath Tala—was renamed as Mujibnagar. Hundreds of Indian and foreign journalists were present at the ceremony when Nazrul Islam took the Guard of Honour as acting President. He appealed to the world for immediate assistance. That evening, Tajuddin, as Prime Minister of the Provisional Government of Bangladesh appealed to the world to recognise the new nation and extend as much material and moral help as possible. He declared, 'Pakistan is now dead and buried under a mountain of corpses. The hundreds and thousands of people murdered by the Army in Bangladesh will act as an impenetrable barrier between West Pakistan and Bangladesh.' He, however, made it clear that any help rendered by any country must be 'free from any desire to control our destinies. We have struggled for too long for our self-determination to permit ourselves to become anybody's satellite.'[5]

The proclamation had a cascading effect. The Deputy High Commissioner of Pakistan in Calcutta, M. Hossain Ali, was the first one to switch his loyalties to the new government.

---

[5] Ibid.

All the 70 members of the Consulate's staff, including the five officers, also transferred their allegiance to the government-in-exile. Two Bengali diplomats in the Pakistani High Commission in New Delhi also defected and were given asylum in India. By the end of the year, about 126 Bengali officials in Pak missions abroad, including Ambassadors posted in Iraq, the Philippines and Argentina, had declared their allegiance to Bangladesh.

In New Delhi, the R&AW was busy processing a flood of inputs coming from Calcutta through different sources but mainly through 'Nath Babu'. RNK had already drafted Maj Gen S.S. Uban, the then Inspector General of the Special Frontier Force (SFF) (the ultra-secret, highly specialised, guerrilla force, mainly comprising Tibetans, which was raised in the midst of the 1962 war with China), to organise Bengali resistance fighters into a cohesive force. While Army Chief, Gen S.H.F.J. 'Sam' Manekshaw was to get the Army HQ to prepare a blueprint for a training programme, the on-ground coordination was to be handled by Maj Gen Uban.

Thanks to Banerjee's knowledge of East Pakistan, and particularly the internal dynamics of the Awami League, the R&AW knew exactly who to support in a bid to get the underground armed movement going, even as it fell on RNK to coordinate the activities of diverse groups within the Bangladesh leadership.

One internal order also formally appointed Banrejee, 'Nath Babu', as the points person for liaison with the political leadership of the provisional government of Bangladesh. In addition, he was to coordinate between the R&AW and the operational headquarters for providing intelligence related to Bangladesh.

Meanwhile, Prime Minister Indira Gandhi, Haksar and Kao had decided to expand the Committee on East Pakistan to now include Defence Secretary K.B. Lall, since sooner or later, the involvement of the Indian armed forces would become inevitable. The Committee was entrusted with the task of overseeing multiple requirements—ranging from decision on giving shelter to important political leaders to installing a radio transmitter and organising armed training to arranging publicity in the media.

Kao's calm and meticulous approach, acquired after years of practicing it as a leader and institution builder, was to prove an invaluable asset in the crucial months ahead as the Indian subcontinent hurtled towards a major crisis.

# TWELVE

# RNK and the R&AW in Top Gear

In 1971, as the summer heat rose in India's capital, so did the political temperature. Bangladesh was on top of everyone's mind. India was still unsure, however, of direct armed intervention in East Pakistan. Instead, RNK and Haksar advocated a campaign that would support the Bengalis who would be at the forefront of the fight back. Prime Minister Indira Gandhi, facing her first international crisis, deferred to their advice and sanctioned the covert operation to be led and coordinated by Kao.

This was to be R&AW's finest hour, thanks to the excellent teamwork at the headquarters, enterprising field operatives led by Banerjee and unstinted support from Mrs Gandhi and her top bureaucrats. Kao's equation with Gen Manekshaw also eventually contributed to India's military success in the 13-day war with Pakistan in December 1971 that helped liberate East Pakistan and created a new nation. The Bangladesh covert operation lasted nearly nine months and kept everyone in the Indian establishment on their toes.

R&AW had to work on multiple fronts. From coordinating movement of Bangladeshi leaders in western countries to organising guerrilla fighters who would operate inside Bangladesh, it had to lead the multi-agency effort. RNK's ability to multitask, assign the right job to the right person and work across ministries to ensure the best outcome possible proved to be a decisive factor in the success of this endeavour. In short, the challenge for RNK, as the man at the centre of the covert operations was to carry all elements of national power with him.

Going by the fragments of some notes, the smattering of correspondence that have survived to this day, and from the reminiscences of many protagonists of the time who penned their memoirs both in India and Bangladesh, RNK emerges as a composed, fully-in-control personality, unruffled by the enormous task on hand, ever ready to be the trouble shooter.

In mid-April of 1971, for instance, RNK had to advice, through foreign secretary T.N. Kaul, India's High Commissioner in London, Appa Pant, how to treat a high-ranking jurist from Dhaka who did not want to return to Bangladesh but was keen to contribute to Bangladesh's freedom struggle. Abu Sayeed Chaudhary, a judge of the Dacca High Court since 1961 and honorary Vice Chancellor of Dacca University, was, however, confused on what could be his exact role. So, he called on Pant at the Indian High Commission. The Indian High Commissioner wrote a detailed letter to then Foreign Secretary, describing Justice Chaudhary as 'utterly sincere and dedicated'. Pant asked Kaul to assess whether 'he [Justice Chaudhary] could become a nucleus of Bangladeshi upsurge abroad and what could be his relationship with other leaders.'[1]

Kaul, on RNK's advice, wrote back to Pant. The Indian High Commissioner was told to help Justice Chaudhary set up an office in London to help Bangladesh affairs to gain greater publicity abroad. The broad principle, RNK advised, of this support should, however, be to make this set-up appear independent, although initial finance would be provided by R&AW. 'His [Chaudhary's] attempt should be to make the whole movement self-supporting on the basis of collections from citizens of Bangladesh and sympathisers. Unless this is done, Chaudhary's cover might be exposed and his credibility as an independent Bangladesh statesman may suffer,'[2] Kaul wrote to Pant after consulting RNK. Kao's observation was because of division and personal rivalries, Bangladesh groups tended to operate independently of one another. Chaudhary was, therefore, told to set himself up as an independent Bangladesh leader at RNK's recommendation.

The Bangladeshi diaspora was to play a major role in mobilising world opinion against Pakistan's atrocities in the eastern Wing. R&AW, while remaining in the background, contributed its bit in coordinating the campaign worldwide. In fact, the Committee of Secretaries had laid down media

---

[1] Indian High Commissioner to the UK, Appa Pant's letter to Foreign Secretary Kewal Singh.

[2] R&AW's internal notes.

publicity as a key task for the R&AW in one of its earliest
meetings. Through its officers, mainly posted in western
countries, the R&AW and MEA made sure that the genocide
that was being committed in Bangladesh would be widely
publicised. Of course, it helped western media, who was also
keen to bring out the horrors of the crackdown in Dhaka and
other towns in Bangladesh.

The Pakistani Army's brutality ensured that the Bengalis,
Hindus as well as Muslims, despite many political differences,
rose as one against Pakistan. R&AW's job was to tap into
the rage. RNK used different agencies and personalities to
harness and coordinate the raw anger amongst the refugees to
create different outfits that would harass and impose a battle
of attrition on the Pakistani forces throughout the summer
and monsoon months of 1971, preparing the ground for the
final assault by the Indian Army, which was brilliantly led by
Sam Manekshaw.

It, of course, helped that RNK, had a very able and
dedicated team in the R&AW. Sankaran Nair was an
admirable foil to RNK. Kao looked at the bigger picture,
attended the meetings at the highest level and left the day-to-
day working of the organisation to Nair. Nair also ran sources
inside West Pakistan and particularly in the highest echelons
of the Pakistani Army which saved the day for India when
the actual war began. But more of that later. Years later, B.
Raman wrote, 'The R&AW's success in East Pakistan, which
led to the birth of Bangladesh, would not have been possible
without the leadership of Kao and the ideas of Nair. The
vision was of Kao and the ideas to give shape to the vision

were largely of Nair. Like Kao, Nair was held in high esteem in the community of international intelligence professionals.'[3]

Meanwhile, RNK's two main links to the Bangladesh Government were two diverse personalities—Banerjee alias Nath Babu and Maj Gen Sujan Singh Uban, the IG of SFF.

Banerjee, as mentioned earlier, was to coordinate and shepherd the diverse personalities and organisations that jostled for influence and dominance in the provisional government of Bangladesh, while Uban, the artillery officer heading Establishment 22 or SFF, would organise armed training for volunteers. The volunteers consisted of a diverse group of Bangladeshi students, farmers, Awami League activists led by Mujib's nephew, Fazlul Haq Moni. It had to be organised into a more disciplined and cohesive force for it to be of any effective use in a guerrilla campaign.

Banerjee and Uban had their own strengths. Banerjee, as the R&AW's Joint Secretary in Calcutta, was the fulcrum around which RNK's political outreach to Bangladeshi politicians revolved. Uban, on the other hand, was the quintessential military trainer, who could take diverse groups of people and forge them into a cohesive guerrilla force capable of operating behind enemy lines.

Uban's task was approved by the Committee of Secretaries for East Bengal in mid-May 1971. He was to initially train the members of the Students League of the Awami League (also known as the Mujib Bahini as they would not have anything to do with the provisional government) at two training centres

---

[3] B. Raman, *The Kaoboys of R&AW* (New Delhi: Lancer Publications, 2007).

established at Tandawa near Chakrata in Dehradun district, and the other at the Halflong SSB training centre in Assam.

The training programme started on 1 June. About 850 selected persons underwent training at the two centres mentioned above. Most of these volunteers were handpicked by the four leaders of the Awami League, who were all close confidantes of Mujib. Uban told RNK, in one of his reports, that he learnt that the Students League was always treated by Mujib as his elite corps. Other Awami League leaders, such as Nazarul Islam and Tajuddin, who were leading the Bangladesh provisional government were only vaguely aware of the existence of the Students League and did not have any detailed knowledge of their activities. The training programme relating to the Students League, along with their identities, were, therefore, kept secret.

RNK had originally envisaged taking the help of the establishment set up by the army to run Operation Jackpot, a separate training programme from the one run by Uban. 'On reconsideration, it is now felt that for various reasons it would be better if we try to do this with our own resources. Action is being taken accordingly,' Kao wrote. As he remarked in one of the reports to the Committee of Secretaries, Kao said, 'In the attached report, IG, SFF, has made some suggestion regarding the operational tasks to be performed by the trained cadres and their cooperation with Army's Operation Jackpot. This involves certain major issues which we shall try to settle first through a separate discussion with the COAS (Chief of Army Staff, Gen Sam Manekshaw) and later at the Secretaries' Committee.'

Uban had been instructed to train up to 6,000 volunteers. Apart from the general training programme, the IG, SFF, was also asked by RNK to have a few teams specially prepared to undertake specific operational tasks relating to targets like the jute mills, the tea industry and the ports in Chittagong and Chalna. 'The training in respect of the targets in and around Dacca is already in progress. For the targets at Chittagong, and Chalna, etc., we had to look for volunteers with local knowledge and the tradition of waterman ship. With the help of the leaders of the Student League such people have also been located, and arrangements made through the clandestine channels to bring them out from East Bengal. It is hoped to start their training by the 10th of July,' Kao informed the Committee of Secretaries on East Pakistan in June 1971.

The specialised training that RNK was talking about had already commenced. It has been documented in detail in a book published during mid-2019, co-authored by the late Captain M.N.R. Samant, Maha Vir Chakra, and one of India's finest defence reporters, Sandeep Unnithan. The book, *Operation X*, chronicles the untold story of India's covert naval war in East Pakistan in 1971.

As Prasad wrote, 'It is noticeable that the nucleus of the Mukti Bahini frogmen was provided by the Bengali sailors, who had deserted the Daphne class submarine Mangro, under construction in France... a few sailors who had been dismissed from service after the Agartala conspiracy case also joined the Mukti Bahini frogmen. In addition, three merchant seamen also merged with this group. Besides the nucleus, 130 frogmen came from Chittagong, 100 from Chalna/Khulna,

40 from Narayanganj... They were essentially tasked to neutralise the main sea ports of Chittagong, Chalna, Khulna and Mongla with a view to prevent logistic support to the Pakistan army... they also aimed to disrupt port operations and prevent export of jute, tea and coir, which earned critical foreign exchange for Pakistan...'[4]

Incidentally, like Banerjee was known to the Bangladeshis as Nath Babu, Kao and Nair too initially concealed their identity. While RNK was simply introduced to the members of the provisional government of Bangladesh as Mr Ram, Nair assumed the name Col Menon. In keeping with the nature of the organisation and its mandate, the R&AW officers were careful in concealing the identities of the Bangladeshi interlocutors too.

Col M.A.G. Osmani, a former colonel in the Pakistani Army but now an elected member of the National Assembly, was appointed the commander-in-chief of the Bangladesh Liberation Army or Mukti Bahini. He was dubbed 'Oliver' by the R&AW. Thereafter, he was always referred to as Oliver in official communication.

As weeks went by, RNK's workload only increased. He had to make sure the secret training programme for the Mujib Bahini proceed without any hitch, act as a trouble shooter when egos clashed, and also advise the prime minister through Haksar.

Often, Banerjee, who had a 360 degree view of the goings on in the Bangladeshi leadership, felt obstructed by the army,

---

[4] S.N. Prasad, *The India-Pakistan War of 1971: A History* (Dehradun: Natraj Publishers, 2014).

especially the GoC-in-C, Eastern Command, Lt Gen Jagjit Singh Aurora, who had his own ideas on how to treat or ignore the Bangladeshi leadership.

For instance, in July 1971, Banerjee sent this report to RNK after spending three hours with Osmani and Tajuddin. First, Banerjee had to make some excuse for Col Menon (Sankaran Nair) not meeting them anymore.

Banerjee wrote, 'Oliver has a lot of complaints against … Aurora. According to him the charge of imparting training to Mukti Fauj was given to the local army authorities early in May. At the very outset Jagjit Singh desired that the EPR & EBR should be disbanded and the members of these organisations as well as other volunteers should be given training only for guerrilla warfare. This was strongly opposed by Oliver and TU [Tajuddin] as they wanted that their people should be trained both in conventional and unconventional methods of warfare and that at least 5 battalions of armed forces should be brought up in inducted into East Bengal…'[5]

He went on to add, 'Oliver feels that in view of the difficulties and the want of rapport between the Bangladesh C-in-C and the Indian army authorities, there is a lot of dissatisfaction, discontentment and misgivings in the Bangladesh army. They've been feeling that the C-in-C is not taking adequate care of the officers and men of the BD Army and is not pressing the Indian army to look after their needs… Certain sections are also of the opinion that the Government of India has adopted a 'go slow' policy and that no efforts are

---

[5] Report of Joint Director, *R&AW*, Calcutta, 3 July 1971, P.N. Haksar papers, File No. 220 (IIIrd instalment), NMML, New Delhi.

being made to increase the efficiency and speed of action of the Bangladesh army ... from the trend of their talks I could see that there was a feeling that Lt. Gen Jagjit Singh Aurora is slighting Oliver and is not giving adequate attention to this urgent demands... Something should be done very quickly to improve the existing relations between the Eastern Command and the Bangladesh army so that the present struggle may not be impeded.'[6]

The moment this input came from Banerjee, RNK apprised Manekshaw of the friction that was developing in Eastern Command and kept Haksar in the loop. Aurora was then told to take corrective action. One can only surmise that these actions were implemented by Aurora, since, in due course of time, the complaints stopped coming. On another occasion, RNK had to mollify Banerjee who felt insulted by a demand from Manekshaw.

A perusal of the exchange of letters between RNK and Banerjee shows that 'Nath Babu' was not happy about Gen Manekshaw wanting the R&AW station in Calcutta to prepare and send daily war bulletins for the Bangladesh Army after receiving inputs from the Indian Army's Eastern Command. Banerjee told Gen Manekshaw that to his knowledge no such decision was taken. 'There was no advantage in routing such materials through the R&AW. We would certainly not like to be the courier of the Eastern Command. Besides, we cannot enter into any correspondence with the BD Government,' Banerjee complained to RNK and requested that he take up the matter with the COAS. He had another point to make.

---

[6] Ibid.

Gen Manekshaw wanted Banerjee to share all the intelligence inputs he sent to Delhi with Eastern Command, which Banerjee refused.

Kao, in his reply, told Banerjee that he would not discuss the matter with Gen Manekshaw. Instead, he instructed the Calcutta station chief to pass onto Gen Aurora relevant portions of the daily intelligence briefs on Pakistan issued by the R&AW. 'No information contained in these reports about West Pakistan should be given to him [Jagjit Singh Aurora],' Kao cautioned Banerjee.

The Calcutta station chief was, however, not happy with RNK's reply. Banerjee again wrote back to Kao asking for clear instructions whether he should continue to act as courier of Eastern Command for this purpose since 'I have to personally handover these bulletins to Oliver since R&AW cannot enter into official correspondence with the BD Government.'

Kao replied immediately saying he had a word with Manekshaw who seemed keen to follow the practice suggested by the army. RNK, therefore, instructed Banerjee to send war bulletins received from Jagjit Singh to the BD Government through the R&AW. 'Perhaps it is not necessary for you personally to go to Oliver to deliver them. "This routine work could probably be done by Bhattacharya (perhaps Banerjee's deputy) or even an SFO or FO, on the days when you are not likely to meet the Bangla Desh leaders",' Kao wrote.

He then pointed out to Banerjee that there were advantages in doing so. Firstly, even in operational matters, the R&AW would continue to have a status and an understanding with the Bangladesh leaders, and secondly, the organisation would see the contents of the war bulletins sent by Jagjit Singh.

This exchange is instructive. As a leader, RNK was looking at the big picture and did not want to quibble on minor issues. At the same time, he managed to make Banerjee see reason and look for positives in a potentially confrontational situation. RNK and Manekshaw maintained an excellent relationship throughout the crisis and later. In one of the exchanges, Manekshaw asked RNK to check if claims made by the Eastern Command about some sabotage operations carried out by freedom fighters inside East Pakistan were correct. Kao replied in detail giving the factual position.

But the R&AW's role was not limited to confirming or denying claims. Banerjee, entrusted to keep a close liaison with the Bangladesh leaders, sent a detailed report in July 1971 to Kao laying bare the divisions, fears and one-upmanship within the provisional government. Banerjee learnt that a majority of the provisional government was unhappy at the manner in which Tajuddin had got himself appointed as the prime minister. No one believed Tajuddin when he claimed that Government of India wanted him to be the prime minister. Otherwise, they (Delhi) would have indicated, he told colleagues in the provisional government. No one believed him and wanted to have a showdown. Despite the anger, Nazrul Islam, the acting President, prevailed upon other members to put aside their differences since fight for Bangladesh was important in his view.

Banerjee then gave his own input on Tajuddin, his background and his standing (or lack thereof) in the Awami League. Tajuddin had no position in the Awami League Parliamentary Party immediately after the elections in 1970. Mujib did not trust him, Banerjee told RNK. In fact, Banerjee had information that on the night of 25 March 1971—when the crackdown happened—Tajuddin, Amirul Islam and Dr Kamal Hossain (an adviser to Mujib on Constitutional matters, who surrendered to the Pakistan Army) had a separate meeting after leaving Mujib's residence. Tajuddin and Amirul Islam, Banerjee wrote in his report, were the first ones to reach the Indian border in the immediate aftermath of the bloodbath and rushed to Delhi to contact the Indian leadership so that Tajuddin could get himself appointed as the prime minister.

On receiving this detailed report, Kao suggested that Nazrul Islam be recognised as the acting President and a monthly meeting between him and Banerjee be held without the knowledge of other ministers to review the situation.

If Banerjee was RNK's primary asset in the Bangladesh political team, Maj Gen Uban played the role of his solution provider in the field. Throughout the nine-month crisis, Uban tirelessly toured the border areas and organised training for over 8,000 men, armed them and controlled their operations inside East Pakistan to harass and weaken the Pakistani Army ahead of the actual war.

Apart from the coordination, supervision, liaising and advice that the R&AW provided to Prime Minister Indira Gandhi and the top leadership that handled the 1971 crisis,

Kao and Sankaran Nair had not forgotten their primary responsibility—that of. providing strategic, actionable intelligence at a critical juncture.

As mentioned earlier, Nair had cultivated a high-grade contact in the Pakistani Army. In the last week of November 1971, one of his moles in Gen Yahya Khan's office informed Nair that the Pakistani Air Force (PAF) was planning a pre-emptive strike on the forward air bases of the Indian Air Force (IAF) in the western sector on the evening of December 1. The IAF was immediately alerted by Nair, and Kao informed this to Indira Gandhi. The IAF was put on high alert and took necessary precautions to thwart the planned pre-emptive strike. Despite the warning, nothing happened on 1 and 2 December.

Air headquarters told Nair that it was impossible for them to keep the pilots in a state of high alert any longer. However, Nair who was very confident about his source, requested the Air Force to continue the alert for another 24 hours and stand down the pilots only after that if nothing happened.

Nair was puzzled. Normally, this source of his was very reliable and accurate. Fortunately, the Air headquarters agreed to continue with the high alert.

Sure enough, on the evening of 3 December, PAF launched its pre-emptive strike on IAF forward bases, which turned out to be a total failure because the IAF had an advanced warning. Later, Nair checked what went wrong. It so happened that the source had sent the correct date—3 December—in his coded message but the decoders at the R&AW messed up.

Fortunately, for Nair and India, this was a mistake that did not prove to be expensive.[7]

A 13-day war, brilliant prosecuted by the Indian military with the help of Bengali liberation fighters IAF, liberated East Pakistan. A new nation was born. Mujib was freed by Yahya. Soon, he took over the reins of Bangladesh.

[7] B. Raman, *The Kaoboys of R&AW: Down Memory Lane* (New Delhi: Lancer Publications, 2007).

# THIRTEEN

# Shepherding Sikkim's Merger

The liberation of Bangladesh was a high point in Indira Gandhi's political career. The success of the operation also sowed the seeds of increased hostility towards India by the US and China. President Richard Nixon and his Secretary of State, Henry Kissinger, were particularly peeved because the 1971 war interfered with their outreach to Communist China via Yahya Khan. China too was annoyed since Pakistan was fragmented and faced a humiliating military defeat.

As Mujib got down to the difficult task of retrieving Bangladesh from the horrors of genocide by the Pakistani Army, Prime Minister Indira Gandhi and her advisers had to be careful to not let the triumph of the 1971 campaign go to their head. There were many challenges to overcome at home. One was staring at them in the face for some years but had been postponed because of the emerging situation in East Pakistan.

That problem arose because of the growing restlessness of the ruler of Sikkim, a protectorate strategically located along the border with Tibet and Bhutan. The Chogyal or the King of Sikkim was increasingly pressurising India to revise the Indo-Sikkim Treaty of 1950, which had granted the tiny Himalayan kingdom the status of a protectorate. Palden Thondup Namgyal, the Chogyal since 1965, mistook India's policy of indulgence towards him as a sign of weakness and started demanding a status for Sikkim on the lines of neighbouring Bhutan.

A bit of background is necessary here to understand Sikkim's history since 1947. Sikkim was one the 600-odd princely states on the eve of India's Independence in 1947. Of these 600, 566 were in the Indian territory, the rest inside Pakistan. Sardar Vallabhbhai Patel, India's first home minister, was the man entrusted with the task convincing the princely states to accede to the newly independent India. Sikkim— like Hyderabad, Junagadh and Jammu and Kashmir—was resisting signing of the instrument of accession that the other 562 princely states had done by 15 August 1947. Patel and his Constitutional advisers were convinced that Sikkim had the same status as the other 562 princely states and should rightly accede to India.

But Jawaharlal Nehru had other ideas. He wanted to grant Sikkim a special status, almost at par with that of Bhutan. Retired Special Secretary of the R&AW and author of a recent book on Sikkim, G.B.S. Sidhu, points out, 'As Sikkim fulfilled the basic criterion of signing the instrument of accession with India, Sardar Patel and BN Rau—Constitutional adviser to the Constituent Assembly—were in favour of treating it on par with the other princely states... Nehru, on the other hand, due to his idealism, Pan Asian Vision and sensitivity to the Chinese concerns in the region, wanted Sikkim to be treated as a special case.'[1]

Nehru moved a separate resolution with respect to Bhutan and Sikkim in the Constituent Assembly to form a separate committee to examine their status with a remark, 'Bhutan is in a sense an independent state under the protection of India. Sikkim is in a sense an India state but different from others.'[2]

That decision, resented by Sikkim's pro-democracy parties, defined India policy towards Sikkim over the next quarter of a century. Sidhu observes, 'This policy, which continued to be followed by the MEA till the end of 1972, revolved around one cornerstone ... that if India wanted to protect its strategic interests in Sikkim, the Maharaja had to be supported under all circumstances to allow him to maintain a firm hold over the administration.'[3] Sidhu, who, as R&AW's points man in Sikkim in the crucial period between 1973 and 1975, describes the policy as a 'mix of apparent appeasement and cautious containment'—appeasement of the Chogyal and containment of the pro-democracy, anti-Chogyal political parties.

By 1972, Indira Gandhi, fresh from her firm handling of the Bangladesh crisis, her political stock as high as it

---

[1] G.B.S. Sidhu, *Sikkim—Dawn of Democracy: The Truth Behind the Merger with India* (India: Penguin Radom House, 2018).

[2] Ibid.

[3] Ibid.

could ever have been, turned her attention to Sikkim. She was frank in admitting, in private, her father's mistake in granting Sikkim the special status. The Principal Secretary, P.N. Dhar—who succeeded Haksar in that crucial post— has noted, 'She [Indira Gandhi] told me in clear terms that her father had made a mistake in not heeding the Sikkimese demand for accession to India in 1947 ... her guess was that he [Nehru] had assumed that the Chinese would leave Tibet Tibet's autonomy undisturbed and, in anticipation of this, he had perhaps thought it fit to do nothing in Sikkim that would provoke them. She had no hesitation in admitting that in retrospect Sardar Patel's instinctive reaction seemed correct. The short point that emerged was that we should undo our earlier mistake and support the people of Sikkim in their struggle against the Chogyal...'[4]

The Chogyal had been emboldened in his new desire to acquire a status similar to Bhutan after a clash between Indian Army and Chinese PLA troops at Nathula, one of the many passes on the border between Sikkim and Tibet in September 1967. Coming as it did, five years after the 1962 debacle, the Chinese probably expected an easy walk-over at the pass. The Indian troops, however, gave a bloody nose to the Chinese and in fact killed many PLA soldiers. The clash nevertheless was a reminder that the border was still vulnerable to misunderstanding and skirmishes and India needed to be on constant guard.

---

[4] P.N. Dhar, *Indira Gandhi, the 'Emergency' and the Indian Democracy* (New Delhi: Oxford University Press, 2000).

Despite its small size (a population of less than 1,30,000), politics and intrigue were very much part of Sikkim throughout the 1950s and the 1960s. While the Chogyal (and his father before him) used their exalted status as the royal family to keep their primacy intact, political parties and leaders opposed to the Chogyal were no less active. The most prominent among the local leaders in the 1960s was Kazi Lendhup Dorji, more popularly known as Kazi or Kazi Sahib, who as leader of the Sikkim National Congress (SNC) fought all his life for a democratic Sikkim.

Added to the mix were two women, both foreigners. Kazi met Eliza-Maria Langford-Rae in New Delhi sometime in the late 1950s. Born in Scotland, raised in Belgium and married to an Anglo-Burmese named Longford-Rae, spent time in Burma (now Myanmar) before surfacing in Delhi's high society circles. Eliza-Maria married Kazi after a brief courtship in 1958. She came to live in Kalimpong thereafter. Both were in their mid-fifties. Kazi's new wife soon took centre stage among Kalimpong's elite. Now called Kazini Sahiba, she was to drive Kazi's political ambitions over the next decade and a half and played a significant part in Sikkim's politically turbulent times.

Hope Cooke, an American, on the other hand, was a young 23-year-old woman who married Thondup, the Choygal in 1963, after a four-year courtship and stayed mostly in Darjeeling's Windamere Hotel where they first met in 1963. The Chogyal's first wife, a local, had died in 1957, leaving behind two sons and a daughter. The Choygal also had a sister, Coocola, who was to also play a significant role in the political developments of the state in the late 1960s and the early 1970s.

Sidhu says the arrival of the women, on either side of the divide, brought a major change in Sikkim's politics and its status in international arena. Hope Cooke started attracting attention in the West. The Kazini too gave the cause of democratisation of Sikkim a greater visibility in Delhi's power circles. As a consequence, Sikkim's status became a topic of animated discussion at a much higher level in diplomatic and political circles. The Choygal's demand for revision of the treaty now became more pronounced.

The ruler of Sikkim had developed ambitions to gain 'independence' for the state. India, sensing the restlessness in the state, had offered an agreement of Permanent Association with India in September 1972 but, according to Sidhu, the Chogyal wanted the offer to include full sovereign rights for Sikkim, a point that India could not have agreed under any circumstances. That is when Prime Minister Indira Gandhi summoned Haksar and Kao to her office. This was end of December 1972. She asked RNK, 'Can you do something about Sikkim?' The R&AW chief asked for a fortnight to revert.

## R&AW Gets into Action

Once again, like in the Bangladesh operation, Kao fell back on P.N. Banerjee in Calcutta. Banerjee met RNK in Delhi and they worked out a plan for Sikkim. The aim was to get the Chogyal to agree to what India had proposed (Permanent

Association) or work for the complete merger of Sikkim with India. Banerjee, who clearly loved action, returned to Delhi in 10 days along with Ajit Singh Syali, who was posted as OSD (P) in Gangtok. Syali was assigned to Gangtok as a R&AW officer primarily to collect trans-border intelligence on Tibet.

The domestic and counter-intelligence duties were left to the IB operatives, after the bifurcation of the IB and formation of R&AW in 1968. Banerjee, as mentioned earlier, continued to hold dual charge on the regional offices of R&AW and IB in Calcutta until his passing away in July 1974.

Banerjee told RNK on his return to Delhi that the ultimate aim of merging Sikkim with India could be achieved and the plan he had worked needed a time frame. Kao took the matter first to Haksar and then to the Prime Minister Indira Gandhi, who gave instant clearance to start the campaign. The only caveat she put was to take Foreign Secretary Kewal Singh on board without giving away the ultimate objective— Sikkim's merger. Singh was to be told that R&AW would work towards undermining and weakening the Chogyal through the agitations launched by political parties led by the Kazi and other younger leaders.

Banerjee and Sayali, who were any way in touch with the political leaders in Sikkim, now had the clearance to encourage them to agitate and demand more powers to the people. Banerjee, with his extensive contacts, and Sayali, because of his familiarity with the situation in Sikkim, rolled out the Operation in early 1973. The timing of launching the operation could not have been better. Throughout 1972 and early 1973, there was heightened unrest in Sikkim because of various local factors. They included massive income inequalities, discrimination against the Nepalese majority and Bhutia-Lepcha highhandedness drawing their strength from proximity to the Chogyal.

An attempt by the palace or elements supporting it to rig the elections of January 1973 added to the problems. This was perhaps the proverbial last straw.

The situation was thus ripe for an uprising against the feudal system, especially the Chogyal. The Kazi was the natural leader for the agitation because of his popularity and acceptance across communities. The Kazi-led SNC joined hands with K.C. Pradhan of the Janata Congress to form a united front against the Chogyal in February 1973. The new front was called the Joint Action Committee (JAC).

It is against this backdrop that Banerjee and Sayali launched their operations. Called 'Janamat' and 'Twilight,' the two operations, going by some of the internal communication, lasted for over two years. They were perhaps codenames given to agitation leaders K.C. Pradhan and the Kazi respectively.

The leaders were met by Banerjee's team in early February 1973.

An update from Banerjee to RNK in early March 1973 said that for the first time since 1949, Sikkim had become a hotbed of tension because of activities of the JAC. There were large-scale protests in different parts of Sikkim and in front of the palace, and boycott of the council by the elected representatives of the Sikkim National Congress ... 'According to reliable sources, the Chogyal has become very much unnerved by the agitation launched by the joint action committee,' Banerjee wrote[5]

Banerjee alerted Kao that one Peter Burley, political officer at the US consulate in Calcutta—who according to Banerjee's assessment was actually a CIA operative—visited Sikkim as a state guest of the Chogyal. During Burley's visit, the Chogyal is reported to have mentioned to him the difficulties being created by the agitators and hinted that he might have to take the help of Government of India to curb the activities of the anti-durbar elements. Another input that RNK received was that the Chogyal was trying to wean away Kazi by negotiating with him after a couple of exclusive, one-on-one meetings with the SNC leader. Banerjee personally was, however, confident that Kazi would not succumb to Chogyal's entreaties because that would mean frittering away a lifetime of support among the people. Banerjee had nevertheless arranged for one of his deputies to meet Kazi at Siliguri around 10 March 1973 to ascertain Kazi's political plans.

In Delhi, the wheels were turning fast. Having decided to remove the protective shield around the Chogyal and support the pro-democracy parties, the PMO, the MEA and the R&AW were all working towards a plan. In a meeting chaired by the newly appointed Foreign Secretary Kewal Singh and attended by the then Defence Secretary K.B. Lall, Home Secretary Govind Narain, RNK, Sikkim's Political Officer, K. Shankar Bajpai, L.L. Mehrotra, Director North in the MEA and Banerjee, who had specially come from Calcutta.

---

[5] Banerjee's note to RNK.

Interestingly, the notes of the meeting, recorded by Banerjee, reveal that the Political Officer had suggested several alternatives to tackle the situation. They included merger with Darjeeling district of West Bengal with some of the districts of Sikkim adjoining Darjeeling and give independence to truncated Sikkim! This was rejected outright.

The high-level meeting, requested by the R&AW, then decided to adopt several measures in the next few months. They were as the following:

1. Strengthen and encourage the agitation till it came to a stage where the Chogyal would be forced to approach Government of India for assistance in dealing with the situation.

2. Devise ways and means to give publicity that the current Chogyal actually had no legal rights to be the King. Thondup's father, Tashi Namgyal, had become King only because his elder brother—the real heir— had voluntarily stepped down. The elder brother's eldest son—Jigmi Taring—should, therefore, have been the real King.

3. Support wide publicity to the agitation throughout Sikkim through local newspapers.

4. Once the agitation gained momentum and the lawlessness increased, send Indian Army troops for occasional route marches to remind the people of their presence.

5. Organise and support big demonstrations when the Chogyal addresses the meeting of the opening day of

the Sikkim Council, which would also be on the 50th birthday of the Chogyal on 4 April 1973.

6.  Make sure that the anti-Chogyal parties and their leaders, especially the Kazi, were told that they would not be abandoned in favour of the Chogyal as it had happened in 1949 when India backed the King instead of democratic forces.

And so it began. The local R&AW team got down to the task of instigating and guiding the agitation, kept the anti-Chogyal leaders united and focused and, of course, offered financial help whenever necessary.

As Sidhu writes, 'By the middle of March 1973, the R&AW's special operations team had started guiding the activities of both the anti-Chogyal parties ... an important challenge that the R&AW's special OPS team had to face at that point was to ensure closer coordination in the functioning of the SNC and Janata Congress, with the ultimate aim of securing their merger into a single party headed by the Kazi. In this respect, of the members of the R&AW's special Ops team, Padam Bahadur, played a significant role. He contacted his old friend SK Rai, general secretary of the Janata Congress, and was finally able to convince him about the virtues of the unity of approach of the two parties to build pressure on the Chogyal to get their demands fulfilled...'[6]

On the day of the Chogyal's 50th birthday, there were clashes on the streets of Gangtok, leading to police firing and a couple of deaths. The Chogyal's elder son, Tenzing, who

---

[6] Ibid.

had ventured out under the protection of the Sikkim guards, was stopped on his way back to the palace. In panic, Tenzing's escort, a captain of the Sikkim guards, opened fire, killing some demonstrators. The Kazi and his party utilised this incident to the hilt by whipping up anti-Chogyal sentiments. By the next day, the tempo of agitation, demonstrations, street marches, some looting and arson had spread across Sikkim.

Back in Delhi, Kao had briefed the prime minister about the imminent takeover by the Indian Government of administration of Sikkim. On 6 April, Indira Gandhi met Foreign Secretary, Kewal Singh, and her Principal Secretary, P.N. Dhar, to seek instructions from her on the situation in Sikkim. Dhar remembers, 'The meeting lasted only about half an hour. Kewal was surprised to find that she had already made up her mind before listening to what he had to say. He guessed that the leaders of the anti-Chogyal moment had kept her informed through R&AW. She was brief and told us that she would accept the Chogyal's request for help as soon as it came...'[7]

Sure enough, it came on 8 April. That day, the Political Officer, K.S. Bajpai, sent one of his First Secretaries, Gurdeep Bedi, to the palace with a draft for the Chogyal. The letter, to be typed on the Chogyal's letterhead, was to be a request by the Chogyal to the Government of India to take control of the administration of Sikkim since there was a complete breakdown of law and order. The letter was to further state that the Chogyal was placing the Sikkim guards and the Commissioner of Police under the Command of GOC,

---

[7] Ibid.

17 Mountain Division of the Indian Army. As Bedi reached the palace, he could see that the Chogyal was sitting in the garden and was conferring with his advisers. Sidhu describes the development thereafter. Soon after, Bedi handed over the draft letter to the Chogyal and explained the purpose of his visit. After reading the draft carefully, the Chogyal exploded, 'Never! I would never place my Sikkim guards under the command of the GOC. He went inside the palace without uttering a single word...'[8]

Chogyal's advisers then went in and out of the palace twice and finally came out to tell Bedi that the Chogyal was ready to sign the draft letter provided he was allowed to retain control of the Sikkim guards. Since telephone lines were dead, Bedi accepted the Chogyal's precondition without being able to take clearance from his boss, Political Officer Bajpai. As the letter was readied, the noise of the anti-Chogyal demonstrations outside the palace was rising by the minute. Bedi, armed with letter, drove out of the palace, lucky not to be stopped or attacked by the crowd since he was in a jeep that had the special number plate assigned to Indian officers and was easily identifiable. Bedi reached the India House at 8 PM and handed over the letter signed by the Chogyal.

The Indian Government had succeeded in its first objective.

The administration was now under Indian control. On 9 April, the Indian Parliament was informed by then minister of state for external affairs, Surenderpal Singh, that 'India would now make every effort to ensure that the interests of the

[8] Ibid.

people are served and safeguarded and that Sikkim marches
on the road to political stability, security and prosperity'.[9]

In Gangtok, satisfied with having achieved his first aim,
Kazi called off the agitation.

## The Next Phase

The MEA selected B.S. Das, an IPS officer of the 1948 batch
from the Uttar Pradesh cadre to become the Chief Executive
of Sikkim. He was briefed thoroughly and told of India's
ultimate objective in Sikkim—the merger of the state to the
Indian Union. The Foreign Secretary told Das that the anti-
Chogyal leaders had to be given full support and assurance
that India was determined to set up a popularly elected
government in Sikkim, and that if the Chogyal resisted, New
Delhi was prepared for a showdown. Das took charge on
10 April.

Within a week, Kewal Singh was in Gangtok, meeting all
sides. The Foreign Secretary met the Chogyal, the prominent
political leaders and, of course, Bajpai and Das. According to
Sidhu, Singh assured the Chogyal of three things:

1. Continuation of the institution of the Chogyal and
   his dynasty with related privileges
2. Parity between Bhutia-Lepchas and the Nepalese
3. Maintain the sanctity of the 1950 treaty

To the JAC leaders, the Foreign Secretary assured
continuation of India's support. He came back again on 7
May to clinch a tripartite agreement the next day.

---

[9] Ibid.

Signed by Kewal Singh, the Chogyal and the political parties led by the Kazi and K.C. Pradhan, the 8 May agreement essentially left the Chogyal with control over the Sikkim guards and the administration of the palace. The centre of gravity had clearly shifted from the Chogyal to Delhi. More importantly, however, it was decided that a legislative assembly to be called a council was to be elected every four years ensuring that no single ethnic group—Nepalese and Bhutia-Lepcha—would have a dominant position. The biggest change was that the Chief Executive, an Indian official, became the virtual chief minister, having the final say in the appointment of ministers and the allocation of their portfolios.

The situation was still fluid though. Banerjee's note to RNK in early May and Kao's own comments on the way forward, sent to Kewal Singh and Dhar, are revealing. Banerjee's note pointed out that the anti-Chogyal movement was continuing in many parts of Sikkim. Processions in the last week of April at several places in South and West Sikkim and a big meeting at Melli by the All Sikkim Youth Congress 'proved the preparedness of the JAC and also its organisational ability,' Banerjee stated. This ended the first phase of the Special Operations launched by the R&AW.

A bigger challenge awaited RNK since Indira Gandhi had made it clear that she wanted a complete merger of Sikkim with India, and in the shortest time possible. RNK's assessment dated 7 May 1973, cautioned everyone, especially the MEA, about the pitfalls of going forward. He noted that the leaders of 'JAC felt that unless constant pressure on the Chogyal is kept up till he goes to the conference table, he may change his attitude any moment'[10]. The Chogyal is bound to exploit differences and mutual suspicion among the political parties, RNK warned and stressed that 'it is therefore necessary that the JAC leaders do not become victims of the Chogyal's machinations'. Kao pointed out that the assurances given by the Foreign Secretary and the Political Officer had raised high hopes in the JAC leaders, and unless a reasonable settlement was arrived at, they may feel frustrated and accuse the Government of India of betrayal.

RNK then goes on to instruct Banerjee about the steps to be taken in the next few months and overcome opposition from within the Indian Government. The task, he said, should be as follows:

1. To give all possible encouragement to the JAC to carry on protracted agitation by staging anti-Chogyal demonstrations and holding big rallies in different parts of Sikkim. Unfortunately, both the PO [Bajpai] and the Chief Administrator [Das] are opposed to this view and both of them are persuading the leaders of the JAC to stop all agitations, and to allow the administration to function normally.

2. It would not be in our interest to allow the Nepalese or other extremist elements of Darjeeling district to join hands with the JAC.

3. We must ensure that in any agreement reached among the various political parties, India's special position in Sikkim is further strengthened.

---

[10] Correspondence between RNK and Banerjee.

4. Neither the Durbar, nor the preponderant Nepalese community, nor the Bhutias/Lepchas should dominate the future set-up of Sikkim. There should be ample scope for us to play one group against the other in future so that no one group becomes too powerful.

5. The negotiations should start, and final settlement must be reached before the restoration of complete normalcy in Sikkim so that we may negotiate with the Chogyal from an advantageous position.[11]

Three days later, Kao, after a long meeting with the Foreign Secretary, sent a long letter to Banerjee tasking him with a few jobs and asking for his opinion on some other measures. 'The intervening period is of critical importance, because every effort should be made meanwhile to keep up and increase the tempo of support for India, and the agitation against Chogyal,' RNK wrote to Banerjee. He also reminded Banerjee that it was necessary to ensure that the Chogyal gets no chance to restart his machinations. 'Our attempt should be to build up such a strength that we are sure of having our candidates returned to at least 70 per cent of the seats in the Assembly,' RNK said.

Kao also instructed Banerjee to ensure that people must be made aware of the disparity in development and progress between Sikkim and the neighbouring districts of West Bengal like Darjeeling so that they start demanding direct representation in the Indian Parliament. Then RNK went on

---

[11] Correspondence between RNK and Banerjee.

to add, 'I need hardly say that during the ensuing months and until the elections are held, our friends should be given assurance of generous financial support.'

As Sikkim appeared headed for more chaos before elections were held over the next six months, RNK wanted to ensure that the momentum of the agitation was maintained. Foreign Secretary Kewal Singh was equally supportive and was ruthless in implementing India's eventual plan to merge Sikkim with India. In response to PO Bajpai's inputs about some inimical activities by the Chogyal's sister Coocoola and her children who were using their contacts in the US and UN circles in New York, 'spreading abusive charges against the Government of India', and their attempts to instigate Bhutia-Lepcha students studying in Delhi against the Government,' Kewal Singh told Bajpai that at 'some stage, she must be made to realise that if she continues to work against India's interests, we shall have to resort to some drastic steps against her.'[12] One of the drastic steps that was thought about was to reopen a case of attempted illegal export of an idol by Coocoola, which was confiscated by the Customs at the Delhi airport. The Indian state, as is well known, can be quite merciless as this case illustrates.

Over the next six months, the R&AW, through Sidhu (who was posted to Gangtok as OSD (P) from August 1973), gradually implemented the next phase of the planned operations. First, elections were held in April 1975. The Kazi won a landslide victory, winning 31 of the 32 seats, going

---

[12] Ibid.

beyond RNK's expectations of winning at least 70 per cent seats! The Kazi now had a legitimate right to go beyond the 8 May 1973 agreement and establish a closer relationship between Sikkim and India. Soon, after much manoeuvring and manipulation, the Kazi could get a new Act—the Government of Sikkim Act, 1974—passed in the Assembly giving Sikkim the status of an associate state. It was now only a matter of time before Sikkim became a full-fledged state of India.

However, there was plenty of drama before the actual merger took place. The Chogyal, on a visit to Kathmandu for the coronation of King Birendra in February 1975, tried to internationalise the Sikkim issue by saying he would approach the UN and demand a free and fair referendum to decide the fate of Sikkim. The Chogyal's behaviour may have finally convinced Delhi to effect the final stage of the plan that had been finalised in December 1972.

While the PO and the MEA prepared the ground for a resolution to be passed in the Assembly, the R&AW had to work behind the scene to make sure that there was no bloodshed or largescale violence. It was essential, therefore, to disarm the Sikkim guards, the Chogyal's loyal soldiers, who could create trouble in the highly charged atmosphere in Gangtok.

Kao left the job to Sankaran Nair.

He drew up an elaborate plan to prepare the ground for justifying the disarming of the Sikkim guards. The scheme is a classic example of what the R&AW could and can do when required. The plan, broadly, was as follows:

1. The disarming of the Sikkim guards should be done on the 8 or 9 of April 1975.

2. Before this action is taken, there should be public meetings and processions in Gangtok demanding removal of the Sikkim guards, complete merger with India and removal of the Chogyal.

3. It should be possible to involve the Sikkim guards in incidents like firing, throwing of hand grenades, etc. Immediately, after these incidents take place, the chief minister and the Cabinet should send a communication to the Chief Executive stating that the Sikkim guards are terrorising the people, and that unless immediate action is taken for their removal from the palace, they will let lose a reign of terror.

4. The news about the incidents by the Sikkim guards and the palace supporters should be on all the ticker tapes at about 8 pm either on 8 or 9 April, for wide publicity in the press.

5. At about midnight, there should be a second handout to the press stating that in view of the prejudicial activities of the Sikkim guards, the PO has asked for help of the army for disarming the Sikkim guards.

6. Next day, after the disarming of the security guards is complete, news should be flashed publicising that the chief minister and the Cabinet have assured that the pay and allowances of all the members of the Sikkim guards would be fully protected and that the Sikkim Government would utilise their services elsewhere.

7. Demonstrations should continue all over Sikkim demanding the full integration of Sikkim with India, and that Sikkim be treated as any other state of India.

8. Resolution should be passed asking for the complete abolishment of the institution of the Chogyal.

9. The chief minister and the Cabinet should assert in a strongly worded resolution that the accession of Sikkim to India was delayed because of the machinations of the Chogyal, and that the people of Sikkim have waited long enough to achieve their desired goal of being part of the mainstream of the life of the country.

10. The Government of India will ask the people of Sikkim to exercise patience. After that, the chief minister should write that he cannot control the upsurge of the people asking for the complete abolishment of the institution of the Chogyal and the complete merger of Sikkim with India.

11. Particular care should be taken that incidents should be credible, publicity should be proper and all possible measures be taken to ensure that the Chogyal does not escape from Sikkim. Every route should be properly guarded, and strong barriers put up. All regular traffic should be thoroughly checked and under no circumstances should the Chogyal be allowed to come out of Sikkim. In case the Chogyal asks for asylum, he should be moved to the India House. After some time, he may be shifted to a suitable guest house about 15–20 miles outside Gangtok with a strong CRP guard

for a period of 15 or 20 days. After the international publicity has died down, negotiations can take place.

The script panned out exactly as planned. Kazi wrote two letters to the Indian representatives—first asking the Sikkim guards to be disarmed and the second, requesting for an emergency session of the Sikkim Assembly.

Accordingly, arrangements were made to employ the army—troops under 64 Mountain Brigade, then Commanded by Brig (later Lt Gen) Depinder Singh—to disarm the Sikkim guards. According to Sidhu, Brig Depinder called the CO of Sikkim guards, Col Gurung, to the 64 Brigade HQ on the morning and kept him there till the end of the operation.

Three army battalions under the 64 Brigade were deployed. Troops marched to the palace and despite one sentry at the gate resisting (he was shot dead), it took less than 20 minutes for the Indian Army to disarm the Sikkim guards. The Chogyal was furious but was helpless. The stage was set for the Emergency Assembly session on 10 April. Kao's Staff Officer, R.T. Nagrani, had meanwhile called Sidhu on telephone to understand how the entire operation was carried out. Events moved fast thereafter.

As planned, the Sikkim Congress issued a statement in Gangtok saying that 'it has now become evident that the people of Sikkim can realise their full rights only if Sikkim becomes a unit of Union of India' The party also called for abolition of the 'oppressive and undemocratic institution of the Chogyal for all times.'[13] On 10 April, correspondence

---

[13] G.B.S. Sidhu, *Sikkim—Dawn of Democracy: The Truth Behind the Merger with India* (New Delhi: Penguin Radom House, 2018).

between the Kazi (his telegram to Mrs Gandhi on 9 April and her response to the Kazi) was released to the media. The denouement was near.

As 10 April dawned, the Assembly met for an emergency session. Twenty-nine Sikkim Congress legislators were in attendance. Two resolutions, one calling for the abolishment of the institution of the Chogyal and Sikkim's merger with India and the second, to hold a referendum on those issues were passed unanimously. Outside, 3,000 odd supporters from distant places in Sikkim arrived in Gangtok and continued to shout anti-Chogyal and pro-Kazi slogans. Kazi was now the new 'king' of Sikkim.

On 11 April, External Affairs Minister Y.B. Chavan made a statement in Parliament referring to the events in Sikkim and justified what had happened. It read, in parts, '… is in the context of the deteriorating law and order situation and the suspicion of the imminent threat to the lives of some leaders in Sikkim that an urgent request was received from the Chief Minister for the immediate disarming and disbanding of Sikkim guards. Even earlier, the Government of India had been approached by the Chief Minister that the Government of Sikkim should not be expected to support with public funds the presence of several hundred armed personnel for the exclusive use of the Chogyal … the evidence of the possible conspiracy against the Chief Minister and his colleagues indicating complicity of some Sikkim guards added urgency to the request, in view of the pressing appeal from the Chief Minister and of the Government of India's responsibility to ensure law and order in the state, the government took necessary steps to disarm the Sikkim guards on the afternoon of 9 April. Before I conclude, I would like to mention another demand by the political leaders in Sikkim, which has been made earlier on many occasions and has been reiterated in recent weeks, for according to the elected government full rights and responsibilities on par with the constituent unit of the Indian union. It is again being repeated, along with the demand for the abolition of the institution of Chogyal in the resolution passed unanimously by the state assembly at its meeting on April 10, the implications of which are being studied by the Government of India.'[14]

Events moved rapidly, and by 15 May—after a Constitutional Amendment Bill incorporating Sikkim as the 22nd state of the Union of India was passed, and after the President gave assent to the bill—Sikkim officially became part of India.

The R&AW's 27-month involvement in the special operations for Sikkim merger officially ended in May. The stellar work done by the officers, first led by Banerjee and then by his successor P.K. Sen in Calcutta, and implemented on ground by A.S. Syali and then G.B.S. Sidhu, directed and controlled from Delhi by RNK and Sankaran Nair, was another feather in the R&AW's cap in less than a decade after it was formed. Kao's already formidable reputation was enhanced further. But soon, in a couple of years, the R&AW was to face its biggest crisis.

---

[14] Ibid.

# FOURTEEN

# The Final Innings

In the intelligence game, there is little scope for practitioners to rest on their laurels or bask in past glory. Having achieved spectacular back-to-back successes in Bangladesh and Sikkim, RNK could have taken it easy; but the geopolitical and security situation is never static, and, therefore, organisations like R&AW have to stay on top of their game all the time.

Post-1962, the Indian intelligence agencies—first the undivided IB and then the R&AW since 1968—had benefitted considerably from their close cooperation with the CIA, especially in strengthening their operational capabilities against China. The setting up of the ARC and the training for SFF were two prime examples; but as the decade of the seventies dawned, the overall relations between India and the US deteriorated. Washington was using Pakistan for its outreach to China. President Richard Nixon and Henry Kissinger used General Yahya Khan to break the ice with the

Chinese leadership in 1972. India was not the most favoured nation in the American capital.

The Nixon administration also had an intense dislike for Mrs Gandhi. As B Raman wrote: 'The hostile attitude of the then US President, Richard Nixon, and his national security adviser, Henry Kissinger, to India, their ill-concealed attempts to prevent an Indian victory (in 1971), the perceived collusion with China ... convinced Indira Gandhi that after Pakistan and China, the US should receive the priority attention of the R&AW... Despite the resignation of Nixon in 1974 in the wake of the Watergate scandal, she felt there is no change in the US hostility to India... She was further convinced that the US hostility was not only to India, but also to her as the Indian leader. She feared that the US intelligence was trying to destabilise her government as a punishment for action in East Pakistan. She started seeing the hand of the CIA everywhere in the setting aside of her election to the Lok Sabha, in the mass movement against her started by Jai Prakash Narayan, in her defeat in the elections of 1977, in the allegations made by the government of Morarji Desai and in the various enquiries ordered by the Morarji Desai government.'[1]

Raman claims that between 1971 and until her death in 1984, the CIA's Psywar Division had launched a vicious disinformation campaign against Mrs Gandhi by using pliant foreign journalists. She was branded a Soviet stooge. The campaign stopped when she was out of power between 1977 and 1980, Raman noted.

---

[1] B. Raman, *The Kaoboys of the R&AW* (New Delhi: Lancer Publications, 2007).

A review of the 1971 operations made it evident to Kao that India still lacked the capacity to have predictive intelligence in the maritime domain, especially the movement of US Naval ships in the Indian Ocean. And, so he set in motion a plan to overcome this shortcoming. Initially, the R&AW set up new monitoring facilities in India's island territories and opening new stations in Indian Ocean countries like Mauritius. The KGB of the erstwhile Soviet Union also tried to help; but it had its limitations in the Indian Ocean. Other countries like the UK, Canada, Japan and Australia were of limited utility because they had close relations with the US. Kao had to look for an effective alternative. So he homed on to the French external intelligence agency, the SDECE.

RNK had correctly assessed that the French, despite their improved relations with the US, continued to be wary of the Americans, and were, therefore, ready to cooperate with the R&AW. The SDECE, then headed by the larger than life personality of Le Comte Alexandre de Marenches, invited RNK to Paris. They hit it off instantly.

The result—setting up of a liaison network between the SDECE and the R&AW to collect real time intelligence on the movement of not only the US naval fleet but also the Soviet ships passing through the Indian Ocean. Raman claims the French spymaster in fact suggested extension of the cooperation by including the Iranian intelligence agency under the Shah of Iran. SAVAK, the Iranian intelligence agency had a good working relationship with the French. Kao accepted the idea since he also knew the Shah personally.

Under the new arrangement, the trilateral cooperation would work like this—the funds would come from the Iranians who would give the money to the French to buy the requisite technical equipment, and India would provide the trained manpower to man the TECHINT stations. The output would be shared by the three nations, it was decided.

Raman said that Kao decided to post him to Paris—under the cover of a journalist for an Indian newspaper—to establish the trilateral network. 'I was selected for two reasons. I had done a course in journalism in the University of Madras in 1956 and worked in the southern editions of *The Indian Express* for four years before joining the Indian Police Service in 1961. I studied French for four years in the Alliance Francaise of New Delhi between 1970–74 and acquired a fairly good working knowledge of the language,' Raman revealed.[2]

Ultimately, however, Raman went to Paris under diplomatic cover and worked there between 1975 and 1979 to kick-start the trilateral cooperation. A couple of monitoring stations were set up on the east and the west coast of India under the project, but soon the arrangement fizzled out because the Shah was toppled by the Islamic revolution in 1979.

Meanwhile, the R&AW had expanded its scope and role rapidly in the wake of the 1971 triumph. New stations were opened abroad despite bureaucratic resistance, operatives were placed in important Indian cities like Madras, Bombay, Calcutta (now Chennai, Mumbai and Kolkata) and in

---

[2] Ibid.

remote border towns and outposts in Ladakh, Sikkim and NEFA (later Arunachal Pradesh). RNK and R&AW were at the zenith. Mrs Gandhi trusted Kao implicitly. Haksar, her Principal Secretary, also supported the newly created organisation, which justified his trust in both 1971 and in Sikkim. Many young men, and, in later years, women, were attracted to the organisation, since it was considered to be an honour to serve in the R&AW.

Kao also started the system of recruiting young men and women directly from colleges and universities post-1971. Four fresh candidates were taken in in 1971—mainly those who were children of known friends and acquaintances, leading to a joke in official circles that R&AW was actually Relatives and Associates Welfare Association.[3]

However, by 1973 it was decided that if the R&AW wanted to pick diverse talent, it needed to have a system of assessing candidates on various parameters before they were recruited. Therefore, from 1973, the second batch of the direct recruits had to undergo a series of tests, interviews and psychiatric evaluation before they could be selected.

Candidates had to fill an exhaustive 35-page form. Thereafter, each candidate was thoroughly investigated: relatives, friends and college teachers, influence, habits— everything was checked out. Then they were called for a series of tests. The first one used to be a psychiatric test. Candidates were called to a place at 3 am or 4 am. It was not the kind of test where all the candidates were tested *en masse*. Once

---

[3] K. Sankaran Nair, *Inside IB and RAW* (New Delhi: Manas Publications, 2019).

the candidate reached there, he was given an objective type test. Thereafter, whoever cleared the test, was called for an individual interview conducted by the Joint Secretary in charge of operations. The next round of interviews, as Jayadeva Ranade (currently, President of the Centre for China Analysis and Strategy and a former Additional Secretary of the R&AW, recruited in 1973) remembers, was with senior officers like NF Suntook and Sankaran Nair who did individual assessments. Once found suitable, they had to face a six-member interview board comprising among others, the Foreign Secretary, the R&AW Chief (Kao) and a psychiatrist. 'I was interviewed for about 45 minutes. The questions were varied and followed no particular sequence: What kind of government India should have; what is the balance of power in the world, etc. Any way, I didn't know how I did, whether I would qualify. I came back to Bombay, where my father was posted. In any case, I had been selected for the Customs Service, so I said to myself, if this doesn't work out, there's always the customs department,' Ranade, who rose to become a China specialist in the R&AW, recalled.

After a couple of months of wait, Ranade was asked to join. Apart from him, three others—Pratap Heblikar, Chakru Sinha and Bidhan Rawal—were part of the 1973 batch of direct recruits. The young officers, after the mandatory training became part of the organisation quickly. 'Kao and Sankaran Nair used to know each and every officer and their background. The organisation had started a "Club 71", where once a month every one used to get together. There was much camaraderie, a sense of belonging. We always felt special. Mr and Mrs Kao were great hosts. Often we youngsters used to double up as bartenders,' Ranade recalled.

Apart from learning the usual craft and science of espionage, each new officer had to learn a foreign language, much like the Foreign Service recruits. Ranade specialised in Mandarin, and is today recognised as one of the foremost Indian experts on China.

R&AW, despite its small size, was seen as a high-performing organisation, important for India's national security. The future looked even brighter. But trouble was lurking round the corner.

## The Difficult Years

1975 turned out to be a landmark year in R&AW's history. Having achieved the merger of Sikkim through a meticulously planned operation, R&AW's stock was as high as it could be. In less than four months, after one of its major success stories, R&AW's prowess, came under scrutiny. Sheikh Mujibur Rahman, the undisputed leader of Bangladesh, was assassinated by a group of junior officers of the Bangladesh Army on 15 August 1975. Almost his entire family, barring the youngest daughter, Hasina, was wiped out in the massacre. India's goodwill in Bangladesh which was at its peak as the immediate aftermath of the liberation of Bangladesh, waned and R&AW came under severe criticism for failing to anticipate or prevent Mujib's killing.

As mentioned in the earlier chapter, Kao was unperturbed about the criticism. It is true that after the sudden death of PN Banerjee alias Nath Babu in a Dhaka Hotel in July 1974,

R&AW had lost contact with the deep and wide network that Banerjee had built in Bangladesh; but it is equally true that Mujib had been dismissive of warnings given to him by R&AW and conveyed to him personally by Kao at least twice and through an intermediary carrying specific inputs from Mrs Gandhi herself. Raman in fact quotes Kao telling him in Paris, 'How can the R&AW be held responsible if Mujib won't take our warnings seriously?'[4] Pupul Jayakar, a close friend of Mrs Gandhi, also quotes RNK in her biography of the late Prime Minister, 'We were walking in the Garden. I told Mujib that we had information about a plot against him. But he was in a state of euphoria. "Nothing can happen to me," he (Mujib) said. "They are my people." This was even though I gave him details of the definite information we had received.'[5]

There was an unexpected fallout after the Mujib assassination in India. Mrs Gandhi, ill-advised by her younger son Sanjay and his cohorts, had declared an internal Emergency in the country after an adverse judgement by the Allahabad High Court declaring her election to Lok Sabha as null and void. Even Kao was unaware of her decision as it was declared all of a sudden. Most Opposition leaders, lawyers and activists were jailed. Mrs Gandhi became paranoid about her own safety. She assumed that the CIA was out to harm her and her family. So, the moment the news of Mujib's assassination came in, Mrs Gandhi was distraught especially

---

[4] Ibid.

[5] Pupul Jayakar, *Indira Gandhi: A Biography* (New Delhi: Penguin Books, 1992).

because Mujib's nine-year-old son, Russell, was ruthlessly killed too. This affected Mrs Gandhi more.

Jayakar writes, 'I went to her house on the evening of 15 August 1975, to find that a great fear had taken her over. Threshold of her insecurity had dropped precipitously. She told me that the assassination of Mujib was the first event in the plot that would submerge the subcontinent. Mujib was the first to go. The next target, she was convinced, would be herself...all manner of primal fears had been aroused.' 'I have disregarded intelligence reports, but I cannot do so any longer,' Mrs Gandhi told Jayakar. 'Rahul (her grandson) was about the same age as Mujib's son. It could be him tomorrow. They would like to destroy my family,' Mrs Gandhi felt.[6] Kao agreed partly. He told Jayakar, years later, 'Mrs Gandhi was the target of attack, not by agents of foreign powers but by Indian recruits who are likely to act as stooges of foreign powers and she was quite right in her suspicion.'[7]

The Emergency, which suspended the Constitution and gave a free rein to Sanjay Gandhi and his supporters to run riot in administration, also created problems for RNK, R&AW and Sankaran Nair. Sanjay Gandhi wanted to see all appointment files, an unconstitutional act in itself since he did not hold any official position in the government.

Just before the proclamation of the Emergency, Mrs Gandhi mentioned to RNK that she wanted to appoint his number two (Nair) as Director, IB. Kao told her that twice previously Nair had refused that post since he was happy

---

[6] Ibid.

[7] Ibid.

being in R&AW. But Mrs Gandhi stuck to her guns. Nair was appointed as DIB, days before the Emergency was imposed. Sanjay Gandhi, who had started going through all the files with the help of Mrs Gandhi's Personal Assistant, RK Dhawan, posed a question: Will the DIB-designate be loyal and carry out all directions implicitly and unquestioningly? Nair wrote: 'Late in the evening, I was summoned to the PM's residence. I refused to go as I had seen her only in office and that too seldom, since she mostly dealt with Ramji. Later, I learnt that Sanjay was extremely annoyed at my refusal to turn up. He had wanted to make sure of my loyalty and pliability, since he was on the verge of getting his mother to declare the Emergency. He took my file to the PM and had her cancel my promotion to DIB. The next day Ramji told me that he was not sure whether to console with me or congratulate me. I said congratulations were in order.'[8]

Throughout the Emergency period, RNK and Nair kept the organisation away from the caucus that had come to rule India in Mrs Gandhi's name, but they could not escape being blamed when the next government came, sweeping Mrs Gandhi aside, electorally. In March 1977, Morarji Desai, became the Prime Minister of the newly-elected Janata Party government. For R&AW and especially RNK, it was the beginning of difficult times.

Senior Ministers in the Janata Party government and the Prime Minister himself had pre-conceived ideas about R&AW. They believed that the organisation was used as a

---

[8] K. Sankaran Nair, *Inside IB and RAW* (New Delhi: Manas Publications, 2019).

private militia by Mrs Gandhi. Kao was to become the first victim of this mistaken belief.

As Nair writes, 'After Morarji Desai became the Prime Minister, he was bent on getting rid of Kao, as head of what he considered R&AW to be Mrs Gandhi's Gestapo. He tried to humiliate Kao every time he went to see him, by mentioning that he had no trust in him. On the third occasion, Kao said he would like to retire prematurely and quit his office. Morarji identified me too, as one of Mrs Gandhi's agents in R&AW. But the Cabinet Secretary, persuaded him to promote me as Secretary R&AW by pointing out that I was one of the founding fathers of the Department. Actually, I was at best, the midwife at the birth of our R&AW.'[9]

But Nair too resigned in less than three months on a matter of principle. The new government wanted to re-designate the Head of R&AW as Director, R&AW instead of Secretary, R&AW. Nair felt this would reduce the importance and influence of the organisation and its chief. Although the Morarji Desai PMO tried to persuade him not to resign, and assured Nair that only the designation was being changed, and that the power and status would remain the same, Nair was not convinced.

With the abrupt departure of the founding fathers, as it were, in close succession, the R&AW in its 10th year of existence, suddenly felt orphaned. 'The entire officer class off the R&AW was saddened by the departure of Shankar Nair. He was a legendary operational officer—totally professional and apolitical, who kept away from all politicians. He was

---

[9] Ibid.

nobody's man. He was a leading expert on the intelligence community of Pakistan and the rest of the Islamic world,' Raman has noted in his book.[10]

However, R&AW was lucky that Kao had groomed others down the line who could become leaders in their own right. One of them was NF Suntook, a naval officer, a policeman, an administrator-turned-spook. Suntook had earlier been shifted to the Joint Intelligence Committee (JIC) from the R&AW by Mrs Gandhi. R&AW was fortunate to have Suntook, as the new chief.

A Parsi from Bombay, Suntook, was initially an emergency commissioned officer in the Indian Navy. After a short stint there, he joined the IPS, shifted to the now defunct Indian Frontier Administrative Service (IFAS)—meant to train and groom administrators for India's northeast—before Kao, who had known about his excellent work in the tribal areas of the north-east persuaded him to join the R&AW at its inception. RNK had made Suntook in-charge of the organisation's Africa Division. He excelled in his work and rose to become number 3 in the organisation before he was deputed to the JIC.

Prime Minister Desai, who had known Suntook in Bombay Police when he was the chief minister of that state, had made a wise choice. Suntook not only steadied the ship but also shielded R&AW from the vendetta that some of the ministers wanted to wreak on the organisation. Old-timers remember Suntook as a low-profile but very effective leader, discreet and polite to a fault. 'Suntook was a man of many

---

[10] B. Raman, *The Kaoboys of the R&AW* (New Delhi: Lancer Publications, 2007).

endearing qualities. He never bragged about himself ... he never talked ill of predecessors ... there was nothing mean about him ... he could have ingratiated himself with Morarji Desai by carrying tales about Kao and Indira Gandhi to him or let himself be used by the new government to witch-hunt Kao or Indira Gandhi or both ... he maintained his personal loyalty to Kao and protected him from possible acts of humiliation ...' B. Raman, then still a serving R&AW officer remembers.[11]

Not that Kao needed protection. Two important ministers in the Morarji government—Home Minister Charan Singh and External Affairs Minister Atal Bihari Vajpayee—had a negative impression about Kao when they took office; but first Charan Singh and then Vajpayee reversed their opinion after a thorough enquiry by the Home Ministry convinced them that Kao had no role to play in the excesses committed during the Emergency. Prime Minister Desai nevertheless imposed a 50 per cent budget cut on the R&AW but Suntook took it in his stride and ran a tight ship.

Kao, reserved and reticent by nature, withdrew from the limelight thrust upon him but he was not out of touch or without influence.

Sometime in 1977, Suntook came to know that attempts were being made in some quarters of the MEA bureaucracy to let India join the Nuclear Non-Proliferation Treaty (NPT), which was against India's interest. Suntook fell back on Kao for help. As it happened, Suntook knew that Dr Homi Sethna, an eminent nuclear scientist based in Bombay, was

---

[11] Ibid.

the only person whose advice Prime Minister Desai would possibly agree to. And the only person who could persuade Dr Sethna to talk to Desai was RNK. Kao and Sethna had worked closely in the late 1960s and early 1970s, throughout Mrs Gandhi's tenure as prime minister, and had struck a great friendship and had high professional respect for one another.

Kao, master at choosing the right person for the right job, sent for Balachandran, who, as mentioned elsewhere in the book, had joined the R&AW in 1975. Kao had noticed his work; he knew that Balachandran during his stint in Maharashtra Police had managed Dr Sethna's security, in the wake of the Pokhran-I period and knew the nuclear scientist well. 'So I was—a relative fresher—sent to Bombay to request Dr Sethna to dissuade the Janata Government from signing the NPT,' Balachandran recounted to me in a conversation in July 2019 at his lovely flat in Mumbai. What transpired between the nuclear scientist and the prime minister is not known but the fact is India did not succumb to international pressure to sign the NPT. And the rest is history. India never signed the NPT. Suntook, Kao and Sethna had saved India from a potential catastrophe. Had India signed the NPT, there would have been no Pokhran II, no nuclear weapons and no nuclear deal with the United States.

Morarji Desai, as prime minister, finally realised the importance of R&AW and strategic Intelligence it provided. But by the time he could start using its expertise, Morarji was ousted after dissensions in the government. However, Desai inflicted a major damage to India's national interest, even if inadvertently.

The story actually goes back to the early 1970s—after the dismemberment of Pakistan—when R&AW picked up fragments of information about Pakistan's attempt to build what it called an 'Islamic bomb'. Kao, in the early years of R&AW, had already set up a Science and Technology Division. By 1977, K 'Sandy' Santhanam, who had joined the R&AW from the Atomic Energy Commission, had concluded, based on several inputs and imagery analysis, that Pakistan was pursuing a military nuclear programme. He was the first to assess that Pakistan had built a uranium enrichment plant at Kahuta. Santhanam and his team kept a close watch on the entire procurement process. Suntook briefed Desai about the development in Pakistan.

The Prime Minister however let it slip in one of his occasional conversations with General Zia-ul-Haq—who had taken over in 1977 as a military dictator after a coup and hanging Bhutto—that India knew of its clandestine nuclear programme. The surprise was lost. Indiscreet political leaders are indeed a bane of intelligence agencies.

### Final Innings

Mrs Indira Gandhi, taking advantage of infighting in the Janata Party and its over-ambitious leaders, stormed back to power, and once again became Prime Minister in 1980. Despite a vindictive streak that her son and she displayed in replacing top officials in agencies such as the CBI and IB, she did not remove Suntook as R&AW chief. It was as much a tribute to Suntook's personality and leadership style as his closeness to

Kao, who was once again back in favour. Mrs Gandhi had started consulting RNK—albeit informally—immediately after becoming Prime Minister again, but it was not until 1981 that she appointed him formally as Senior Adviser in the Cabinet Secretariat. Kao made sure that Suntook, who had shielded him from a witch hunt in the Janata Party regime, continued as R&AW Chief. However, according to Raman, neither RNK nor Suntook, could prevent four senior officers of the organisations from being victimised for perceived and imaginary sins of commission and omission.

According to Balachandran, Mrs Gandhi appointed Kao as Senior Adviser after ACN Nambiar—journalist, freedom fighter, close friend and associate of Jawaharlal Nehru and Subhash Chandra Bose—advised her in 1981 during their meeting in Zurich to do so. Nambiar, who doted on Mrs Gandhi, was worried about her security and wanted Kao back as her adviser. Balachandran, then posted in Paris, was specifically instructed to look after Nambiar—'Nanu' to everyone—and make sure he was comfortable in the twilight of his life.[12]

Kao was back on a salary of Re 1 (*see photo of his appointment letter*). It helped that Suntook was still heading the R&AW. Their rapport was intact. After taking over as Senior Adviser, Kao, resumed some of the half-done tasks during his tenure as the founding Chief of R&AW. The first was to revive RAS. To get the recruitment right, Kao asked

---

[12] Vappala Balachandran, *A Life in Shadow: The Secret Story of ACN Nambiar, A Forgotten Anti-colonial Warrior* (New Delhi: Roli Books, 2016).

Sankaran Nair, his former number two to recommend how to fix the inter-se seniority of officers from different services and the direct recruits in the RAS. Nair's recommendations were accepted and the RAS was reconstituted.

The second important decision Kao took was to constitute the Policy and Research Staff (PRS), which can rightly be called the forerunner to the National Security Council Secretariat (NSCS), formed in 1999. Three R&AW officers and one Indian Foreign Service Officer worked in PRS to give crucial inputs to the R&AW Chief and the Prime Minister.

One of the many security challenges that stared India in the face after Mrs Gandhi returned to power was the rising discontentment in Punjab fuelled by the pro-Khalistani elements. It did not help that Mrs Gandhi's own Home Minister, Zail Singh, was playing games with the Punjab problem. Aware of the potential danger it posed to India, Kao advised Mrs Gandhi to initiate dialogue with the saner elements among the Punjab leadership but despite several rounds of talks at the political level between Rajiv Gandhi and his associates and Akali Dal leadership on the one hand, and Kao and some Khalistani elements abroad, on the other, the Punjab problem seemed intractable.

Eventually, Mrs Gandhi ordered the army into the Golden Temple, the holiest shrine of the Sikhs, triggering widespread anger among Sikhs worldwide—even among the moderate ones. She instantly became a target of the extremist elements in the Khalistani movement. Kao, aware of the potential danger, tried to strengthen her security. Sikh bodyguards in her security detail were removed; Kao ordered an ambulance to be part of her convoy and also requested her to wear a bullet proof vest. Inexplicably however, the instructions that no Sikh bodyguard should be part of her inner security ring, were disregarded. On 31 October 1984, two of her Sikh bodyguards shot Mrs Gandhi in her house, taking revenge for what they believed was her unpardonable act of sending the army into the Golden Temple and the desecration of the Akal Takht.

Mrs Gandhi's brutal end was a big blow to Kao personally and professionally. RNK was, in fact, not in India the day Mrs Gandhi was killed. He was in Beijing—under Mrs Gandhi's instructions—for a making secret overtures to the Chinese leadership in an attempt to normalise the relationship between India and China. When the Chinese heard of the assassination, they offered to place a special plane at Kao's disposal for him to reach India as soon as possible. RNK's standing with the Chinese enabled him to reach Hong Kong in the special aircraft and from there travel in a commercial flight to Delhi.

Kao must have returned to India a devastated man. He had failed to protect Mrs Gandhi—whom he had known closely for over three decades, initially as Nehru's daughter, and later, as a prime minister who did not hesitate to take hard decisions—and, his own reputation as an intelligence Czar. But true to his style, RNK never spoke or wrote about his own feelings. He quietly faded away, leading a fully retired life, but never out of touch with contemporary issues in the field of intelligence as his correspondence with Balachandran in later years—1998 to 2000—showed. In one of the letters, RNK wrote to Balachandran on the need for better coordination and analysis, '...It is not enough either for the IB or the R&AW to send intelligence reports to the government. Someone with adequate experience has to interpret these reports to the government. In 1981, before I was appointed in the Cabinet Secretariat as Senior Adviser, in briefing me, the late Mrs Indira Gandhi, had said to me, amongst other things, that the intelligence organisations by themselves "did not see the wood for the trees". I made a small beginning to remove this deficiency, but other events intervened, and the whole venture was aborted.'

The setback in his second innings notwithstanding, Rameshwar Nath Kao will forever be remembered as a colossus in the world of Indian intelligence, more an institutional builder than an operative, more of a spymaster than a spy. And a gentleman to the core.

# Appendix

TOP SECRET IMMEDIATE
C-in-C
BANGLADESH FORCES
GUERILLAS – ORGANISATION, EQUIPMENT
AND EMPLOYMENT
AIM OF INSTRUCTION

To ensure guerillas coming out of training establishments are inducted on a planned basis in all sectors, these instructions covering the following, are issued:

(a) Organisation, Arms and Equipment of Guerillas
(b) Phased Induction of Guerillas

## Organisation

**Basic Organisation.** The basic organisation is a section of 1 Guerilla leader and 7 guerillas, having a total of eight who can be split into two cells each of three to four guerillas on an as required basis. Several Sections would be constituted into a platoon under a platoon leader who will be assisted by a deputy leader. Similarly several (3 to 5) platoons would be constituted into a Guerilla Company which will be led by a Company Leader. A company leader would have a political adviser carefully selected by the Bangla Desh Forces Sector Commander on the advice of the Civil Liaison Officer attached to him. The political adviser will advise the Guerilla Company Leader on all political and internal developments inside the areas of operation and also motivate guerillas in meeting day to day developments. Indoctrinated locals will normally be used for courier duties. Intelligence net-work will be organized through local agents. At a selection level there will be no separate intelligence cell, but at platoon level there will be an intelligence cell of 3 well-trained guerillas. In addition, there will be a trained Nursing Attendant. Similarly at a company level there will be eight well-trained guerillas to form an intelligence section, besides a doctor and 3 nursing attendants. For specific areas requiring it, an anti-tank detachment and other supporting light weapons detachments shall be attached. All guerillas, including their units/sub-units, shall come under the command of the Bangla Desh Forces Sector Commander concerned who will coordinate operational tasks. The only exception will be those operating under HQ Bangla Desh Forces on special tasks who will be provided with special identity cards for identification in friendly areas. For organisation see Appendix 'A' attached.

## Arms, Equipment and Dress

### Arms

(a) Individual Weapons

| | |
|---|---|
| Leaders | Pistol, firing single and automatic shots, preferably 9 mm with a magazine enabling it to be used as a carbine also |
| Deputy Leaders | Pistol 9 mm |
| Guerillas in a Section | • Four with carbines machine sten 9 mm which must be capable of firing single rounds also<br>• Two with Rifles<br>• One with LMG |
| Nursing Attendants with platoon and Company HQ | Rifles |
| Guerillas on intelligence duties at Platoon and Company HQ | • 25% Pistols 9 mm<br>• 75% Carbine Machine Sten<br>• 9 mm (Must be capable of firing single rounds also) |
| Anti Tank Detachment - 4 Guerillas | • 50% Pistol<br>• 9 mm<br>• 50% Rifles |
| Every Guerilla | Two hand grenades and a double edged knife with a 6 in to 9 in double edge blade |

(b)  For each company: A detachment of 4 guerillas equipped with 2 rocket launchers (3.5 in or 40 mm of equivalent to deal with gun boats, bunkers, fuel/amn dumps, etc., shall be provided in areas where it is considered necessary.

## *Equipment*

(a)  Section:
     One complete demolition kit preferably US origin.
     One first-aid box.
(b)  Platoon: Adequate medical and surgical (dressing/cleansing/kit for the Nursing Attendant to provide preliminary attention to the casualties at a hidden 'safe house'. Medical kit must include anti-venum serum and syringe for administration in case of snake bite.
(c)  Company: Adequate medical/surgical equipment and supplies for treating casualties at a well-hidden 'safe house' which should serve as a temporary hospital.

## *Dress*

Guerillas will be dressed in ordinary civilian clothes of a coarse type conforming to those commonly worn in the locality. Uniformity in colour or design must be strictly avoided. Mosquito/insect repellant oil shall be carried for use at night. Scale of clothing/necessaries to be issued shall be restricted to:

| | |
|---|---|
| Civilian type ground sheet | 1 |
| Vests | 2 |
| 'Gamcha' | 1 |
| Lungi | 1 |
| Pyjama | 1 |
| Civilian type water proof sheet (to cover oneself against heavy rain) | 1 |
| Cheap rubber shoes (pair) | 1 |
| Soap | 1 |
| Shirt or 'Kurta' | 1 |

**Supplies:** Apart from the pay Rs 50 (fifty) per month guerillas will be provided with rations. Whenever necessary, edible items of the type of haversack pack rations shall be provided.

# Phased Induction of Guerillas

## *General Instructions*

(a) Immediately on completion of training, guerillas should be grouped keeping in view areas with which they are fully conversant (preferably they should have their homes in the area). The area of operation of different guerilla units/sub-units/individuals should be clearly defined using Stich natural features as rivers, 'Khals', hills, etc.

(b) Guerillas will be launched and all their operations conducted through the Bangla Desh Forces' Sector Commanders in conformity with these instructions. To assist in the training and in the training and in the conduct of guerilla operations, a GW Team from HQ Bangla Desh Forces, consisting of one or more of the following officers shall tour and maintain regular liaison with training centres and Sector Commanders and offer advice on the organisation employment of guerillas:

  (i) Capt Shariful Haq, Arty

  (ii) Lieut Matiur Rahman, E Bengal

  (iii) Lieut S.H.M.B. Nur Chowdri, E Bengal

(c) Guerillas will be issued with arms/equipment as prescribed in these instructions by the Sector Commanders, prior to employment on tasks.

## *Phased Induction*

(a) Phase I: Establishment of Firm Bases Inside.

  1. Time: Task to be completed earliest. Progress will be intimated by Sector HQs through GW LOs being sent from Bangla Desh Forces HQ. Supporting HQ will be kept in picture.

  2. Task to be carried out:

    (i) Area analysis or detailed analysis of the terrain and situation inside the area.

    (ii) Establishment of own intelligence network and clanaestine communication system (with alter native arrangements) to higher headquarters end other guerilla sub-units in the area.

(iii) Establish contact with own cells operating inside on similar mission.

(iv) Establishment of secure clandestine routes of infiltration and exit.

(v) Organisation of logistics for own operations based on local resources.

(vi) Selection of 'cache' sites and 'safe houses'.

*Notes:*

1. During this phase it is essential to maintain absolute quiet (lying low and underground) and peace in the area to avoid suspicion and detection by enemy agents. Hence liquidation of enemy agents must NOT be attempted inside the area at this stage but all information about them collected. Nor should any force be used in the interior during this phase. Instead, diversionary activities combined with elimination of enemy agents should be carried out far away, along the border areas.

2. There must be several alternative secret bases, alternative communication system and clandestine routes organised to prevent detection of any one.

(b) Phase 2: Unbalancina and Weakening the enemy.

1. Time: Task to be completed soonest, after completion of Phase.

2. Tasks to be carried out: In this phase the enemy's liability to operate has to be destroyed by a series of well-planned and vigorous (daily growing in tempo) guerilla strikes over a wide area in which there will be great need for the utmost pre-thought, secrecy and skill as the enemy will be in control of the area at the beginning of the phase. The specific tasks to be completed by the guerillas will include:

(i) Liquidation of enemy agents, informers and collaborators.

(ii) Destruction of the enemy's means of communication including destruction of telecommunications, rail/road bridges, removal of fish plates from railway lines, removal of navigation marks on inland water ways/rivers, disruption/denial of ferry's on roads, destruction of river ports and jettys and ambushing enemy while trying to disembark troops/stores on river banks.

(iii) Denying the enemy all resources by destruction of POL depots, refineries power supply (by destroying pylons/sub-stations).

(iv) Destroying the enemy's fighting power and transport by planned ambushes on his road/rail/river lines of communication, and raids on small targets like arms/ammunition/POL/supply depots, river and road transports and small posts.

(v) Destroy or render ineffective air base facilities and aircrafts.

(c) Phase 3: Knocking out the last breath (from the enemy)

   1. Time: As soon as the enemy has been incapacitated and he no longer has the ability to strike.

   2. Tasks to be carried out: In close conjunction with the, regular forces to destroy the already bled and incapacitated enemy and secure liberated areas. In this the guerillas' particular tasks (to be coordinated by the Bangla Desh Forces Sector Command concerned) will be to attack the enemy's flanks, rear, his supporting arms and destroy his communications so that he is disabled from concentrating his fire power or switching his forces, thus facilitating the task of his destruction.

(d) Phase 4: Consolidation and Restoration

   1. Time: On collapse of the enemy government.

   2. Tasks to be carried out: The main task will be one of consolidation of liberation and restoration of own civil government and administrative authorities. In this the guerillas' main tasks will be to carry out the following in close conjunction with the regular forces:

     (i) Elimination of any enemy elements still holding out.

     (ii) Assist the quick restoration of normal public life.

     (iii) Conversion from a guerilla force to a People's Army (2nd line Army) and resettlement of personnel (not desirous of continuing in regular forces) in civil life, to include resumption of education by those whose education was disrupted by the war.

**For c-in-c**

**Distribution List:**

| Copy No. | Addressee | |
|---|---|---|
| 1. | Comd Sector 1 | |
| | Comd Sector 2 | through LO |
| | Comd Sector 3 | |
| | Comd Sector 4 | |
| 2. | Comd Sector 5 | |
| | Comd Sector 6 | through LO |
| | Comd Sector 7 | |
| 3. | Comd Sector 8 | through LO |
| | Comd Sector 9 | |
| 4. | Files for the use of Staff own HQ | |
| 5. | Comd Alpha Sector—Supporting Forces | |
| 6. | Comd Bravo Sector—Supporting Forces | |
| 7. | Comd Charlie Sector—Supporting Forces | |
| 8. | Comd Delta Sector—Supporting Forces | |
| 9. | Comd Echo Sector—Supporting Forces | |
| 10. | Comd Foxtrot Sector—Supporting Forces | |
| 11. | Comd Own Supporting Forces. | |